Sarah Salmon is a barrister at Cornerstone Barristers. She specialises in public law, housing and property. Called to the Bar in 2007, her work has involved all aspects of housing law and she regularly advises both local authorities and applicants on homelessness and allocations.

Sarah is ranked as a leading junior in Legal 500 for both Administrative Law and Human Rights and housing where she has been described as "simply exceptional". She is also recommended in Chambers and Partners for housing.

A Practical Guide to Housing Allocation Schemes in England

A Practical Guide to Housing Allocation Schemes in England

Sarah Salmon, LLB (Hons), LLM, Barrister

Law Brief Publishing

Published 2024 by Law Brief Publishing, an imprint of Law Brief Publishing Ltd
30 The Parks
Minehead
Somerset
TA24 8BT

www.lawbriefpublishing.com

Paperback: 978-1-916698-07-9

PREFACE

The purpose of this practical guide is to give readers an overview of social housing allocation in England. Part 6 of the Housing Act 1996 makes provision for how local authorities allocate housing. This book looks at the provisions of Part 6 as they apply in England. The area is complex and local authorities face challenges as social housing stock is in high demand and low supply. Allocation schemes, designed to shape how a local authority allocates housing, and how they are applied to individual circumstances are often ripe for challenge by way of judicial review.

This book should allow its readers to understand the basics to navigate Part 6 of the Housing Act 1996 and seeks to be a useful initial reference guide for those working within social housing, their lawyers and students. The law in this book is believed to be correct and up-to-date as at 31 March 2024.

I have had some assistance at the very end of this process and would like to thank Sarah McKeown and Susan Salmon for helping to proofread the final version. I would also thank Garry Wright, Law Brief Publishing and my husband for their patience.

Sarah Salmon
March 2024

CONTENTS

INTRODUCTION

The general management, regulation and control of housing stock by a local authority is vested in, and to be exercised by, that authority by virtue of section 21 of the Housing Act 1985. The management and allocation of housing stock is, however, subject to certain statutory constraints. One of those constraints is Part 6 of the Housing Act 1996 which makes provision for how local authorities allocate housing. This book looks at the provisions of Part 6 of the Housing Act 1996 as they apply in England.

The legislative scheme

On 24 July 1996, the Housing Act 1996 obtained Royal Assent. Part 6 of that Act has governed the allocation of social housing in England and Wales from around 1 April 1997.[1] Local housing authorities shall comply with Part 6 when allocating housing accommodation[2] but, subject to the provisions within Part 6, a local housing authority has a discretion as to how they allocate social housing accommodation.[3]

Since 1997, Part 6 has gone through some important changes. First, it was modified by sections 13 to 16 of the Homelessness Act 2002.

- Section 13 removed the general prohibition that the provisions of Part 6 did not apply to a person who was already a secure or introductory tenant, an assured tenant (but not an assured shorthold tenant) of housing accommodation held by a registered social landlord (now known as a private registered provider of

---

1 Article 3, Housing Act 1996 (Commencement No.5 and Transitional Provisions) Order 1996/2959.

2 Section 159(1), Housing Act 1996.

3 Section 159(7), Housing Act 1996.

social housing in England), or an assured tenant of housing accommodation allocated to him by a local housing authority by replacing those provisions with a subsection (5) that provided Part 6 does "*not apply to an allocation of housing accommodation to a person who is already a secure or introductory tenant unless the allocation involves a transfer of housing accommodation for that person and is made on his application*".

- Section 14 abolished the duty to maintain a housing register and inserted section 160A regarding the allocation of housing accommodation to persons that are eligible.

- Section 15 dealt with information, advice and assistance being available from a local housing authority to persons in their district.

- Section 16 amended how a scheme should be framed in respect of priorities and those to whom a reasonable preference should be given.

Secondly, approximately ten years later, in England, Part 6 was extensively amended by sections 145 to 147 of the Localism Act 2011. These changes came into force on 18 June 2012.[4] The amendments by the Localism Act 2011, do not apply to Wales save for some minor amendments required due the divergence between how housing accommodation was to be allocated in England and Wales. It is the position after the changes in England by the Localism Act that will be discussed throughout this book.

Finally, there have been some recent minor amendments to sections of Part 6 (both applying to England and Wales), from 1 December 2022,

---

[4] Article 3, Localism Act 2011 (Commencement No.6 and Transitional, Savings and Transitory Provisions) Order 2012/1463.

necessitated by the wholesale changes to social housing/landlord and tenant law in Wales made by the Renting Homes (Wales) Act 2016.[5]

Allocating housing

Local housing authorities must have a scheme for determining priorities and procedures in relation to the allocation of social housing and must allocate such housing in accordance with that scheme.[6] How a scheme is put together is governed by Part 6 of the Housing Act 1996, relevant regulations and statutory guidance made pursuant to section 169 of the Housing Act 1996. Readers will see, when looking at Part 6 of the Housing Act 1996, there are areas of difference between the statutory provisions in England and Wales. As set out at the beginning of this introduction, this book deals with the provisions as they apply to England only.

In England, the main statutory guidance – *Allocation of accommodation: guidance for local authorities* – was first published in June 2012 and last updated on 15 May 2023 ("the statutory guidance for local authorities"). Readers are able to see all the amendments and keep an eye on any future amendments through the GOV.UK website.[7] There is other statutory guidance on narrower issues of allocation which shall be addressed within this book.

When framing any allocations scheme, local housing authorities should also consider caselaw and various other statutory regimes, for example,

5 For information about those changes you can see Law Brief Publishing's, *Renting Homes: The New Law of Letting in Wales* by David Smith (January 2023).

6 See generally, sections 166A and 167, Housing Act 1996 in relation to England and Wales respectively.

7 As at the date of this book, the current link to the guidance is: https://www.gov.uk/guidance/homelessness-code-of-guidance-for-local-authorities.

the Equality Act 2010, the Children Act 1989 and the Domestic Abuse Act 2021.[8]

The purpose of this practical guide

The purpose of this practical guide is to give readers an overview of social housing allocation in England. The area is complex. Allocation schemes and how they are applied to individual circumstances are often ripe for challenge by way of judicial review which some of the cases mentioned throughout this book demonstrate. This book should, however, allow its readers to understand the basics to navigate Part 6 of the Housing Act 1996 and seeks to be a useful initial reference guide for those working within social housing, their lawyers and students.

8 An in-depth analysis of such statutory schemes is outside the scope of this book but Law Brief Publishing does offer practical guides in many other areas, *for example,* readers can go to "A Practical Guide to the Public Sector Equality Duty in Housing" by Nick Bano (February 2023) and "A Practical Guide to Housing Law and the Domestic Abuse Act 2021" by Yinka Adedeji (October 2023).

CHAPTER ONE

THE APPLICATION OF PART 6 OF THE HOUSING ACT 1996

Local housing authorities

As set out in the introduction to this book, Part 6 applies to local housing authorities who "shall comply" with it.[9]

When does Part 6 not apply to an allocation of social housing?

A housing allocation scheme decides who is eligible for social housing and the condition applicants are required to meet. Part 6 of the Housing Act 1996, however, sets out some parameters as to the types of allocation that Part 6 applies to. Importantly, the provisions within Part 6 do not apply in the following circumstances.

Part 6 does not apply to a person who is already: (a) a secure or introductory tenant[10] of a local authority, or, (b) an assured tenant in

9 Subsection 159(1), Housing Act 1996.

10 A local authority or a housing action trust may elect to operate an introductory tenancy regime.

relation to accommodation held by a private registered provider of social housing[11] ("PRPSH") or a registered social landlord[12] ("RSL") unless:

- the allocation involves a transfer of housing accommodation for that person,
- the application for the transfer is made at the request of that person, and
- the local housing authority is satisfied that the person is to be given reasonable preference under section 166A(3), Housing Act 1996.[13]

This means that in the circumstances described above, any application to transfer to other accommodation by an existing secure, introductory or assured tenant of a local authority or PRPSH/RSL, as the case may be, where the tenant has a reasonable preference for an allocation, must be treated in the same way as any allocation under Part 6 of the Housing Act 1996. Reasonable preference will be discussed later in this book.

---

11 The Housing and Regeneration Act 2008 created the concept of private registered providers of social housing. This is a term apply in England only. Section 80 of the Housing and Regeneration Act 2008 explains how "provider of social housing" is to be construed and, thereafter, how the words "registered providers" and "private registered providers" are applied. On the most basic level, this term refers to social landlords in England who are not local authorities.

12 Again, on the most basic level, this is how social landlords in Wales are referred to. When the Housing and Regeneration Act 2008 created PRPSHs in England, it restricted the "registered social landlord" system to Wales. Prior to these changes, social housing providers in England were also known as RSLs.

13 Subsections 159(4A) and (4B), Housing Act 1996.

As confirmed by paragraph 1.6 of the statutory guidance for local authorities, this means that a local housing authority can retain flexibility in setting policies that deal with all other types of transfer. This will include circumstances where a local housing authority offers a management transfer (because such a transfer is initiated by the local housing authority rather than the tenant it would fall outside of the scope of section 159(4B) of the Housing Act 1996).[14]

A management transfer, sometimes referred to as a management move, allows someone to be allocated a property outside the allocation scheme despite the fact there may be others on the waiting list that would qualify for such an allocation. Local housing authorities will have policies dealing with circumstances within which management transfers can be considered and/or made. Such circumstances may include moving tenants where they, or their household, have particular needs arising from a disability. It may also include moving tenants where they, or their households, are at a risk of violence, for example, where someone is at risk from gang violence. In addition, whilst a local housing authority should take account of situations involving domestic abuse when creating its housing allocations scheme, management transfers, which would not be a Part 6 allocation, are also used where a tenant, or a member of their household, has been subjected to domestic abuse. A decision not to accommodate on the basis of a management transfer could be the subject of a claim for judicial review: see, for example, *R (on the application of*

[14] It should be noted that whilst a local housing authority should take account of situations involving domestic abuse in its housing allocations scheme, management transfers, which would not be a Part 6, Housing Act 1996 allocation, are also likely to be relevant where an applicant has been subjected to domestic abuse. A decision not to accommodate on the basis of a management transfer could be the subject of a claim for judicial review: see *e.g. R (on the application of TRX) v Network Homes Ltd* [2022] EWHC 456 (Admin); [2023] HLR 6.

TRX) v Network Homes Ltd [2022] EWHC 456 (Admin); [2023] HLR 6.

Another common circumstance which will not be a Part 6 allocation is where a local housing authority has to temporarily decant (*i.e.* move someone out of their home on a temporary basis) a tenant and their household to do repairs.[15] Such a temporary move should mean that the tenant and their household move back into their home one works are carried out. Again, local authorities are likely to have policies and procedures in place for temporary moves due to disrepair.

The flexibility, provided because of how Part 6 operates, allows local housing authorities to decide how best to manage their social housing stock and respond to urgent circumstances of need. This is important when there are huge pressures on social housing and is something local authorities are best placed to do.[16]

Part 6 of the Housing Act 1996 will also not apply where an introductory tenancy becomes secure following the end of the introductory trial period or any trial period extended in accordance with section 125A of the Housing Act 1996[17] (a trial period can be extended by 6 months if certain conditions are met). So long as any trial period is not extended, the duration of an introductory trial period is the period of 12 months (or one year) starting from the date on which the tenancy was entered into or the date, if such a date is later, on which a tenant was entitled to

[15] See the statutory guidance for local authorities at paragraph 1.9.

[16] See *e.g. Harrow London Borough Council v Qazi* [2004] 1 AC 983, 997, para 25; *Manchester City Council v Pinnock* [2010] UKSC 45; [2011] 2 AC 104 at [54]; *London Borough of Hounslow v Powell* [2011] UKSC 8; [2011] 2 AC 186 at [35] and *Thurrock Borough Council v West* [2012] EWCA Civ 1435; [2013] HLR 5 at [25].

[17] Subsection 160(3)(a), Housing Act 1996.

possession under the tenancy. Being entitled to possession is likely to be the date upon which a tenant can move into a property.[18]

Further, Part 6 will not apply where a secure or introductory tenancy:

(a) has been succeeded to following the death of the tenant with the tenancy consequently vesting in the successor under section 89 of the Housing Act 1985 (secure tenancy) or section 133 of the Housing Act 1996 (introductory tenancy);[19]

(b) is assigned (*i.e.* transferred) to a person who would be qualified to succeed the secure or introductory tenant if the tenant had died immediately before the assignment; or

(c) vests (*i.e.* given to someone else) or is otherwise disposed of in pursuance of:

    (i) a property adjustment order in connection with matrimonial proceedings under section 24 of the Matrimonial Causes Act 1973 or section 17(1) of the Matrimonial and Family Proceedings Act 1984,

    (iii) an order for financial relief against parents under paragraph 1 of Schedule 1 to the Children Act 1989, or

    (iv) a property adjustment order in connection with civil partnership proceedings or after overseas dissolution of

---

[18] Section 125, Housing Act 1996. There is also provision in section 125 regarding the trial period where a tenancy is adopted by a local authority or housing action trust or where an introductory tenant was formerly a tenant under another introductory tenancy. Such detail is outside the scope of this book.

[19] The complexities of succession are outside the scope of this book. For further details, see Law Brief Publishing, *A Practical Guide to Succession to Social Housing Tenancies* by Stephanie Lovegrove (March 2023).

civil partnership, etc. under Part 2 of Schedule 5, or paragraph 9(2) or (3) of Schedule 7, to the Civil Partnership Act 2004.[20]

In relation to secure tenancies, there are some additional circumstances set out in subsection 160(2) of the Housing Act 1996 where the provisions of Part 6 will not apply. The first is where a tenancy remains secure pursuant to section 90 of the Housing Act 1985. Section 90 of the Housing Act 1985 applies where a secure tenant dies and the tenancy is a tenancy for a term certain. A "term certain" is not defined in the Housing Act 1985 but is a term used throughout a variety of legislation and is part of the common law. Despite its long term use, relatively recently, in *Livewest Homes Ltd (formerly Liverty Ltd) v Bamber* [2019] EWCA Civ 1174; [2019] 1 WLR 6389, after a review of its use, case law and Blackstone's Commentaries on the Laws of England, the court held at [59] that the word "certain" means that the lease (or tenancy) was granted for a term expressed to expire on a certain dated rather than on an an uncertain date. What section 90 of the Housing Act 1985 provides for is what happens to such a tenancy where the secure tenant dies. Part 6 does not apply to such circumstances.

The other two circumstances are referred to generally as mutual exchange *i.e.* where a secure tenancy:

(a) is assigned (*i.e.* transferred) by way of exchange (*i.e.* a swap of homes/tenancies) under section 92 of the Housing Act 1985; or,

(b) is granted in response to a request under section 158 of the Localism Act 2011. In brief, this is where a tenancy is exchanged by ending the existing tenancy and granting a new tenancy in the circumstances that are set out in section 158 of the Localism Act 2011.

---

20 Subsection 160(2) and (3), Housing Act 1996.

In addition, section 160 of the Housing Act 1996 provides a power for the Secretary of State to make regulations as to when Part 6 will not apply.[21] The relevant regulations are the Allocation of Housing (England) Regulations 2002.[22] Regulation 3 provides that Part 6 does not apply in the following cases.

(a) Where a local housing authority secures the provision of suitable alternative accommodation pursuant to its duty to rehouse residential occupiers under section 39 of the Land Compensation Act 1973. Section 39 of the 1973 Act sets out a duty to rehouse residential occupiers when they are displaced from any land as a consequence of certain actions of a local authority using various powers local authorities have to acquire, improve, redevelop, or make orders in relation to, land, houses and/or buildings.

(b) The grant of a secure tenancy to a former owner-occupier or statutory tenant of a defective dwelling-house under sections 554 and 555 of the Housing Act 1985.

(c) Accommodation let by a local housing authority on a family intervention tenancy.[23]

When Part 6 applies – the meaning of "allocation"

Finally, section 159(2) of the Housing Act 1996 also sheds some light on the circumstances in which Part 6 applies (or will not apply). Section 159(2) sets out what an "allocation" is. Part 6 only applies to an allocation as defined by this section. Section 159(2) provides that, for the

---

21 Subsections 160(4) and (5), Housing Act 1996.

22 SI No. 3264.

23 Family intervention tenancies were introduced by the Housing and Regeneration Act 2008 (section 297) and are not secure or assured tenancies (see schedule 1, Housing Act 1985 and schedule 1, Housing Act 1988).

purposes of Part 6, a local housing authority allocates housing accommodation when they:

> *"(a) select a person to be a secure or introductory tenant of housing accommodation held by them,*
>
> *(b) nominate a person to be a secure or introductory tenant of housing accommodation held by another person,*
>
> *(c) nominate a person to be an assured tenant of housing accommodation held by a private registered provider of social housing or a registered social landlord,*
>
> *(d) select a person to be a tenant under a secure contract[24] or an introductory standard contract[25] of housing accommodation held by them, or*
>
> *(e) nominate a person to be a tenant under a secure contract or an introductory standard contract of housing accommodation held by another person".*

Selecting a person to be (a) a secure tenant; or, (b) a tenant pursuant to a secure contract; or, (c) a tenant under an introductory standard contract, includes circumstances where a local housing authority exercises any power to notify an existing tenant or licensee that their tenancy or

24 Secure contracts are one of the types of tenure available under the Renting Homes (Wales) Act 2016. Whilst this book does not cover the provisions relating to the allocation of accommodation in Wales, there could be circumstances where a local housing authority in England has cause to nominate someone to be a tenant under a secure contract. It should be noted that in Wales, those holding secure contracts are known as contract-holders rather than tenants.

25 Introductory standard contracts are a type of tenure available under the Renting Homes (Wales) Act 2016.

licence is to be of a type set out at (a) to (c) of section 159(2).[26] Selecting a person in such circumstances will include, for example, where a local housing authority notifies an applicant that a tenancy granted pursuant to any homelessness function under Part 7 of the Housing Act 1996 where the local authority is the landlord will be secure. In the ordinary course of things, such a tenancy is not a secure tenancy.[27]

Nominating a person to be a secure or introductory tenant of housing accommodation held by another person is an allocation. So too is nominating a person to be an assured tenant of housing accommodation held by a PRPSH or RSL or a tenant under a secure contract or an introductory standard contract of housing accommodation held by another person. It does not include nominating a person to be an assured shorthold tenant.[28] The reference to nominating a person to be a certain type of tenant within section 159(2) will also include *"nominating a person in pursuance of any arrangements (whether legally enforceable or not) to require that housing accommodation, or a specified amount of housing accommodation, is made available to a person or one of a number of persons nominated by the authority"*.[29]

The definition of an allocation makes it clear that there will be other circumstances relevant to local housing authorities that will fall outside the Part 6 regime as it only applies where someone is selected or nominated to be a secure, introductory or assured tenant or a secure or introductory standard contract holder. Whilst this may cover the majority of scenarios, there are other obvious examples, in addition to the circumstances already outlined above, where there will not be an "allocation". Such examples include where temporary accommodation is being provided to a homelessness person under a non-secure tenancy

---

26 Subsection 159(3), Housing Act 1996.

27 See paragraph 4, schedule 1 of the Housing Act 1985.

28 Subsection 159(2)(c), Housing Act 1996.

29 Subsection 159(4), Housing Act 1996.

agreement and where an agreement is granted under the Mobile Homes Act 1983.

Is an allocation the same as granting a tenancy?

It is important to recognise that an allocation is not the same as a local housing authority granting a tenancy. In *Birmingham City Council v Qasim* [2009] EWCA Civ 1080; [2010] PTSR 471, the Court of Appeal considered Part 6 of the Housing Act 1996 (prior to the Localism Act 2011 amendments) and, as part of that consideration, asked itself whether or not an allocation under Part 6 include the grant of a tenancy. The Court of Appeal held that Part 6 of the Housing Act 1996 was:

> *"18. …concerned with, indeed limited to, establishing and then managing priorities between applicants for residential accommodation (which may or may not be owned by the local authority in question) as it becomes available for letting, which effectively is preliminary to, and not part of, the actual letting of such accommodation, which is governed by Part II of the 1985 Act".*

Whilst acknowledging at [20] that distinguishing an allocation (under Part 6, Housing Act 1996) and a disposal (under Part 2, Housing Act 1985) in such a way may be *"artificial"* and *"rather technical"*, in checking the analysis worked, the Master of the Rolls pointed to:

(a) the use of the words "select" and "nominate" within section 159(2); and,

(b) the fact that in some cases the rules under Part 6 do not apply under what is now subsection (4A), (4B) and (5) of section 159 and section 160, and held that the procedure in the legislation for selecting an applicant to be a secure tenant of available accommodation was not a purported disposal by way of the grant of a secure tenancy.[30]

What is the consequence of granting a tenancy to a person not selected in accordance with Part 6 of the Housing Act 1996?

This was the second question considered in *Birmingham City Council v Qasim* [2009] EWCA Civ 1080; [2010] PTSR 471. It was held that, whilst housing is to be allocated in accordance with a local housing authority's allocation scheme, as the grant of a secure tenancy is different to deciding whether a person should be allocated accommodation, *"the grant of a secure tenancy by an authority to someone to whom accommodation has been allocated inconsistently with the authority's scheme does not thereby render the tenancy void or ineffective"*.[31] On the most basic level *Qasim* confirms that a tenancy will be valid in circumstances where it has been granted to a person that was not selected or nominated in accordance with a local housing authority's allocation scheme.

30 *Birmingham City Council v Qasim* [2009] EWCA Civ 1080; [2010] PTSR 471 at [21]-[24].

31 *Birmingham City Council v Qasim* [2009] EWCA Civ 1080; [2010] PTSR 471 at [25]-[37].

CHAPTER TWO

ELIGIBILITY FOR AN ALLOCATION UNDER PART 6 OF THE HOUSING ACT 1996

Part 6 of the Housing Act 1996 contains rules for the allocation of accommodation by local housing authorities to those persons that are eligible and/or qualify for such an allocation. This is the first main area of Part 6 where there are separate sections covering the rules governing England and Wales. For England, readers first need to consider section 160ZA of the Housing Act 1996 which was added by the Localism Act 2011.[32] This chapter considers the basic provisions in relation to eligibility.

Who is eligible for an allocation of housing?

Eligibility is complicated. It can involve questions of immigration status which can leave the best of us scratching our heads. It is also subject to change on a relatively regularly basis especially given the state of some parts of the World. For example, recent changes include provisions as to those coming to the UK from the Ukraine and Sudan.[33] The complexities

---

32 In force from January 15, 2012 for purposes specified in article 4(1)(k) of the Localism Act 2011 (Commencement No.2 and Transitional and Saving Provision) Order 2012/57 (subject to transitional and savings provisions specified in arts 6, 7, 9, 10 and 11 SI 2012/57) and from June 18, 2012 otherwise.

33 See the Allocation of Housing and Homelessness (Eligibility) (England) and Persons Subject to Immigration Control (Housing Authority Accommodation and Homelessness) (Amendment) (No. 4) Regulations 2022/1371 reg.2(2) (January 30, 2023) (Ukraine) and Allocation of

of immigration law are outside the scope of this book but this section aims to highlight the relevant provisions to which those making decisions and their advisors will need to have regard.

It is important to get questions about eligibility right. This is because a local housing authority in England is expressly prohibited from allocating housing accommodation to a person from abroad who is ineligible.[34]

It should be noted that the eligibility criteria do not apply to anyone who is already an introductory or secure tenant of a local authority or an assured tenant of a PRPSH or RSL. As discussed in chapter 1, many situations that arise in relation to such tenants fall outside the scope of Part 6 of the Housing Act 1996. Where matters are within scope – *i.e.* where an existing secure, introductory or assured tenant requests a transfer and the local housing authority has to be satisfied that the person is to be given reasonable preference for an allocation[35] – subsection 160ZA(5) makes it clear that the provisions as to eligibility in subsections 160ZA (1) to (4) do not apply.

Subject to what has been set out above, the restrictions in place as to eligibility for an allocation of social housing do apply to individual applicants as well as to any joint application (where at least one person is ineligible). Section 160ZA(1)(b) makes it clear that a local housing authority shall not allocate housing accommodation to two or more

---

Housing and Homelessness (Eligibility) (England) and Persons Subject to Immigration Control (Housing Authority Accommodation and Homelessness) (Amendment) Regulations 2023/530 reg.2(2) (May 15, 2023) (Sudan).

34 Ground 5 of schedule 2 to the Housing Act 1985 (tenancy by deception) may allow a local authority to regain possession of a property when a false statement has been made knowingly or recklessly as part of a Part 6, Housing Act 1996 application: see *e.g. Oshin v Greenwich RBC* [2020] EWCA Civ 388; [2020] PTSR 1351.

35 Subsection 159(4B), Housing Act 1996.

persons jointly if any one of them is a person from abroad who is ineligible. As the guidance for local authorities highlights, however, this does not mean that ineligible persons cannot form part of an eligible applicant's household:

> *"...a housing authority must not grant a joint tenancy to 2 or more people if any one of them is a person from abroad who is ineligible. However, where 2 or more people apply and one of them is eligible, the authority may grant a tenancy to the person who is eligible. In addition, while ineligible family members must not be granted a tenancy, they may be taken into account in determining the size of accommodation which is to be allocated".*[36]

A person from abroad will be ineligible if they are subject to immigration control within the meaning of the Asylum and Immigration Act 1996 and they do not fall within a class prescribed by regulations made by the Secretary of State.[37] The prescribed classes are the exceptions to the general position. The legislation provides, however, that no one who is excluded from an entitlement to universal credit or housing benefit because of section 115 of the Immigration and Asylum Act 1999 shall be included in any class prescribed.[38] An applicant will be a *"person subject to immigration control"* if they are a person who under the Immigration Act 1971 requires leave to enter or remain in the United Kingdom.[39] This is whether or not such leave has been given.[40]

---

36 Paragraph 3.4 f the of the Allocation of accommodation: guidance for local authorities.

37 Section 160ZA(1) Housing Act 1996 and paragraph 3.6 of the of the Allocation of accommodation: guidance for local authorities.

38 Subsections 160ZA(1) to (4), Housing Act 1996.

39 Section 12(2), Asylum and Immigration Act 1996. Please note below in relation to EEA citizens.

40 Section 12(2), Asylum and Immigration Act 1996.

A person from abroad will also be ineligible if they are classed as ineligible for an allocation by the Secretary of State.[41] Such classes will be prescribed by regulations. The relevant regulations are the Allocation of Housing and Homelessness (Eligibility) (England) Regulations 2006 ("eligibility regulations").[42] As alluded to above, the regulations, which came into force on 1 June 2006, have been amended on a number of occasions. In relation to the allocation of social housing, the main provisions are found within regulations 3 (those persons subject to immigration control who are eligible for an allocation) and 4 (those who are ineligible for an allocation). Regulations 3 and 4 need to be read with regulation 2 which is the regulation dealing with interpretation.

Classes of persons from abroad who are eligible

Regulation 3 of the eligibility regulations defines a number of classes of person who are persons subject to immigration control but are eligible for an allocation of housing accommodation under Part 6 of the Housing Act 1996. There are currently 16 classes running from A to P. The classes (the wording for which has primarily been taken from regulation 3) are as follows.

- **Class A** refers to a person who is recorded as a refugee by the Secretary of State and has leave to enter or remain in the United Kingdom. This means the person will fall within the definition in Article 1 of the Refugee Convention. The Refugee Convention is a reference to the Convention and Protocol relating to the Status of Refugees incorporating the text of 1951 Convention (Geneva, 18 July 1951) and the 1967 Protocol (New York, 31 January 1967).[43] Article 1 of the Refugee Convention sets out a single definition as to whom the term "refugee" shall apply. The

41 Subsections 160ZA(1) to (4), Housing Act 1996.

42 SI No. 1294.

43 Regulation 2, eligibility regulations.

guidance for local authorities explains that a person granted refugee status is normally granted 5 years' limited leave to remain in the United Kingdom.[44]

- **Class B** applies to a person who has exceptional leave to enter or remain in the United Kingdom which has been granted outside the rules laid down in section 3(2) of the Immigration Act 1971 ("the immigration rules")[45] and who is not subject to a condition to maintain and accommodate themselves, and any person who is dependent on them, without recourse to public funds. The guidance for local authorities sets out that usually "discretionary leave" is the form exceptional leave to remain now takes.[46]

- **Class C** means a person who is habitually resident[47] in the United Kingdom, the Channel Islands, the Isle of Man or the Republic of Ireland and whose leave to enter or remain in the United

44 Paragraph 3.14(i) of the Allocation of accommodation: guidance for local authorities.

45 See regulation 2(1) of the eligibility regulations. The rules are those laid down (and amended) before Parliament by the Secretary of State from time to time via a statement of rules: section 3(2) Immigration Act 1971.

46 Paragraph 3.14(ii) of the Allocation of accommodation: guidance for local authorities.

47 "Habitually resident" is a phrase seen within a few of the prescribed classes. There is guidance at paragraphs 3.20 and 3.21 and Annex 2 of the Allocation of accommodation: guidance for local authorities as to the test to be applied and factors to consider. Decisions will turn on the specific facts of any case but, in brief, there must be a link between the person and their place of residence. The guidance for local authorities suggests that where a person is continuously resident for a period of two years (temporary absences may be disregarded) prior to an application for housing then they are likely to be "habitually resident". Local housing authorities are encouraged to make further enquiries where the period of two years has not been established.

Kingdom is not subject to any limitation or condition will be eligible for an allocation of social housing. Class C does not, however, include a person:

(a) who has been given leave to enter or remain in the United Kingdom upon an undertaking given by his sponsor (a sponsor is a person who under the immigration rules has agreed by way of an undertaking – *i.e.* a promise – in writing to be responsible for the accommodation and maintenance of another person[48]);

(b) who has been resident in the United Kingdom, the Channel Islands, the Isle of Man or the Republic of Ireland for less than five years beginning on the date of entry or the date on which his sponsor gave the undertaking in respect of him, whichever date is the later; and

(c) whose sponsor or, where there is more than one sponsor, at least one of those sponsors, is still alive.

The guidance for local authorities explains that where the sponsor or all of the sponsors (if there was more than one) have died within the first five years then an applicant will be eligible for an allocation of accommodation.[49]

- **Class D** are those who have humanitarian protection. Such protection is given to a person under the immigration rules.[50]

---

48 Regulation 2, eligibility regulations.

49 See paragraph 3.14(iii) of the Allocation of accommodation: guidance for local authorities.

50 The immigration rules can be found at https://www.gov.uk/guidance/immigration-rules. It is a lengthy

- **Class F** relates to a person who has been granted limited leave to enter or remain in the United Kingdom on family or private life grounds under Article 8 of the Convention for the Protection of Human Rights and Fundamental Freedoms. This leave to enter or remain is that which is granted under paragraph 276BE(1), paragraph 276DG or Appendix FM of the immigration rules. Class F will apply so long as the person is not subject to a condition to maintain and accommodate themself and any dependent without recourse to public funds.

- **Class G** applies to person who is habitually resident[51] in the United Kingdom, the Channel Islands, the Isle of Man or the Republic of Ireland if that person has been transferred to the United Kingdom under section 67 of the Immigration Act 2016 (unaccompanied refugee children) and has limited leave to remain under paragraph 352ZH of the immigration rules (which sets out what the Secretary of State must be satisfied of to grant such leave to remain).

- **Class H** will be a person who is habitually resident[52] in the United Kingdom, the Channel Islands, the Isle of Man or the Republic of Ireland and has Calais leave to remain. The Home Office has published guidance for caseworkers regarding Calais leave[53] which is given to a person under paragraph 352J of the immigration rules. The Home Office guidance explains that Calais leave is only available to unaccompanied children who

---

document. In relation to Humanitarian protection, paragraph 3.14(iv) of the Allocation of accommodation: guidance for local authorities sets out that the relevant rules are 339C to 344C.

51 See footnote 16 above.

52 See footnote 16 above.

53 Calais leave: Caseworker guidance, published 3 December 2018 and last updated on 31 December 2020.

were, between 17 October 2016 and 13 July 2017, transferred to the United Kingdom in connection with the clearance of the Calais camp. It goes onto explain that those granted Calais leave, and their dependants, will have received a residence permit with a validity of 5 years. At the end of the 5 year period, if the person renews their Calais leave, they will be given a further residence permit, valid for 5 years. After a period of 10 years' continuous leave in the United Kingdom, a person may apply for indefinite leave to remain.[54]

- **Class I** provides eligibility where a person has been granted limited leave to enter or remain in the United Kingdom in accordance with Appendix EU of the immigration rules. In short, this class applies where the person is a family member of a "relevant person" of Northern Ireland under the immigration rules. Under Appendix EU of the immigration rules, a relevant person of Northern Ireland is *"a person who:*

  (a) is:

    (i) a British citizen; or

    (ii) an Irish citizen; or

    (iii) a British citizen and an Irish citizen; and

  (b) was born in Northern Ireland and, at the time of the person's birth, at least one of their parents was:

    (i) a British citizen; or

---

54 Page 5 of the Calais leave: Caseworker guidance, published 3 December 2018 and last updated on 31 December 2020 which can be found at: https://assets.publishing.service.gov.uk/government/uploads/system/uploads/attachment_data/file/947797/calais-leave-v3.0ext.pdf.

(ii) an Irish citizen; or

(iii) a British citizen and an Irish citizen; or

(iv) otherwise entitled to reside in Northern Ireland without any restriction on their period of residence".

- **Class J** is a stateless person who is habitually resident[55] in the United Kingdom, the Channel Islands, the Isle of Man or the Republic of Ireland and who has limited leave to remain in the United Kingdom. Such leave is given under paragraph 405 of the immigration rules and can be given for a period not exceeding five years. Whilst certain persons are excluded from being recognised as a stateless person; a stateless person is essentially someone who is not recognised as a national by any State under its laws.[56]

- **Class K** – within the immigration rules there is an Appendix that deals with "Hong Kong British National (Overseas)". This is what Class K is concerned with. A person will be eligible for an allocation under Class K if they are habitually resident[57] in the United Kingdom, the Channel Islands, the Isle of Man or the Republic of Ireland and have been given limited leave to enter or remain in the United Kingdom under Appendix Hong Kong British National (Overseas). Class K will not apply, however, if the person's leave to enter or remain is subject to a condition that the person has to maintain and accommodate themselves, and

55 See footnote 16 above.

56 See Article 1(1) of the 1954 United Nations Convention relating to the Status of Stateless Persons.

57 See footnote 16 above.

any person dependent upon them, without recourse to public funds.

- **Class L** is concerned with two categories of person who come to the United Kingdom from Afghanistan.

  The first category is a person who has been granted leave to enter or remain in the United Kingdom in line with the immigration rules, where such leave has been granted because of: (a) the Afghan Relocations and Assistance Policy; or (b) the previous scheme for locally-employed staff in Afghanistan.

  The second category is a person with leave to enter or remain in the United Kingdom that does not fall within the first category and who has left Afghanistan in connection with the collapse of the Afghan government on 15 August 2021. The second category does not, however, include a person who is subject to a condition that they have to maintain and accommodate themselves, and any person dependent upon them, without recourse to public funds. It also does not include a person who has been given leave to enter or remain in the United Kingdom where an undertaking has been given by a sponsor in relation to being responsible for the applicant's accommodation and maintenance and the person has been resident in the United Kingdom, the Channel Islands, the Isle of Man or the Republic of Ireland for less than five years. The calculation of the five years either begins on the person's date of entry or on the date on which their sponsor gave the undertaking, whichever date is the later. In addition, the sponsor or at least one of them (if there was more than one) must still be alive.

  Class M was introduced in relation to the war in Ukraine. Someone will fall into Class M if they are a person in the United Kingdom who immediately before 1 January 2022 was residing in Ukraine and left in connection with the Russian invasion on

24 February 2022. The person will also have to have been granted leave under the relevant immigration rules.

- **Class N** also relates to persons from the Ukraine. It covers those who have limited leave to remain which has been granted pursuant to the Appendix Ukraine Scheme of the immigration rules where the application has been made by that person from within the United Kingdom.

  As with some of the other classes already set out, a person will be excluded from **Classes M and N** if they are subject to a condition as part of their leave to maintain and accommodate themselves, and any person who is dependent upon them, without having recourse to public funds.

- **Class O** provides eligibility to a person who has limited leave to remain granted in accordance with Appendix Temporary Permission to Stay for Victims of Human Trafficking or Slavery of the Immigration Rules.

- **Class P** applies to a person who was, prior to 15 April 2023, residing in Sudan. It applies in circumstances where they have left Sudan in connection with the violence in Khartoum and across Sudan that rapidly escalated on 15 April 2023. The person also has to have leave to enter or remain in the United Kingdom given in accordance with the immigration rules and must not be a person:

  (a) whose leave is subject to a condition requiring that person to maintain and accommodate themself, and any person who is dependent upon them, without recourse to public funds; and

  (b) who has been:

(i) given leave upon an undertaking as to responsibility accommodation and maintenance given their sponsor;

(ii) who has been resident in the United Kingdom, the Channel Islands, the Isle of Man or the Republic of Ireland for less than five years beginning on the date, whichever is later, of entry or the date on which the sponsor gave the undertaking; and

(iii) whose sponsor or one of them (where there is more than one) is still alive.

Classes of persons from abroad who are ineligible

As set out above, it is regulation 4 of the eligibility regulations that provides for other persons from abroad who are ineligible for an allocation of housing. Regulation 4 deals with persons who are not subject to immigration control. If such a person falls within one of the descriptions set out below, a local housing authority will not be able to allocate housing to them under Part 6 of the Housing Act 1996.

The first type of person described who will be ineligible is someone who is not habitually resident[58] in the United Kingdom, the Channel Islands, the Isle of Man, or the Republic of Ireland. This description is, however, subject to a number of exceptions. Even if someone is not habitually resident as required, they shall not be treated as ineligible for an allocation of housing accommodation if they are:

[58] See footnote 16 above.

(a) a worker (which has the same meaning as for the purposes of "qualified person" in regulation 6(1) of the Immigration (European Economic Area) Regulations 2016[59]);

(b) a self-employed person (which has the same meaning as for the purposes of "qualified person" in regulation 6(1) of the Immigration (European Economic Area) Regulations 2016[60]);

(c) a person who is a worker within the meaning of "qualified person" in regulation 6(1) of the Immigration (European Economic Area) Regulations 2016 pursuant to regulation 5 of the Accession of Croatia (Immigration and Worker Authorisation) Regulations 2013. The Immigration (European Economic Area) Regulations 2016 are referred to within the eligibility regulations as "the EEA Regulations" and, regulation 2 of the eligibility regulations, provides that references to the EEA Regulations are to be read with schedule 4 to the Immigration and Social Security Co-ordination (EU Withdrawal) Act 2020 (Consequential, Saving, Transitional and Transitory Provisions) Regulations 2020;

(d) a person who is a family member of those people who would fall within (a) to (c) above. References to the family member of a worker or self-employed person shall be construed in accordance with regulation 7 of Immigration (European Economic Area) Regulations 2016. Although under this category of person, a family member does not include a person who is to be treated as a family member under regulation 7(3) of the Immigration (European Economic Area) Regulations 2016;[61]

---

59 Regulation 2(2), eligibility regulations.

60 Regulation 2(2), eligibility regulations.

61 Regulation 2(2) and (3), eligibility regulations.

(e) a person with a right to reside permanently in the United Kingdom under regulation 15(1)(c), (d) or (e) of the Immigration (European Economic Area) Regulations 2016;

(f) a person who as a result of their deportation, expulsion or other removal by compulsion of law from another country is in the United Kingdom;

(g) a frontier worker (*i.e.* a person within the meaning of regulation 3 of the Citizens' Rights (Frontier Workers) (EU Exit) Regulations 2020);

(h) a person who is a family member of a frontier worker and has a right to reside having been granted limited leave to enter or remain in the United Kingdom under Appendix EU to the immigration rules. References to the family member of a frontier worker shall be construed in accordance with regulation 7 of Immigration (European Economic Area) Regulations 2016. Although under this category of person, a family member does not include a person who is to be treated as a family member under regulation 7(3) of the Immigration (European Economic Area) Regulations 2016;[62]

(i) a person who in connection with the collapse of the Afghan government on 15 August 2021 left Afghanistan;

(j) a person who immediately before 1 January 2022 was living in the Ukraine and left in connection with the Russian invasion on 24 February 2022; or,

62 Regulation 2(2) and (3), eligibility regulations.

(k) a person who before 15 April 2023 was residing in Sudan and left in connection with the violence on 15 April 2023 in Khartoum and across Sudan.

The second type of person is someone where their only right to reside in the United Kingdom is derived from their status as a jobseeker or as a family member of a jobseeker. Jobseeker has the same meaning as for the purposes of "qualified person" in regulation 6(1) of the Immigration (European Economic Area) Regulations 2016).[63] References to the family member of a jobseeker person shall be construed in accordance with regulation 7 of Immigration (European Economic Area) Regulations 2016.[64]

The third type of person is someone where their initial right to reside in the United Kingdom is for a period not exceeding three months under regulation 13 of the Immigration (European Economic Area) Regulations 2016.

The fourth type of person that will be ineligible is someone who has a derivative right to reside in the United Kingdom the entitlement for which comes from regulation 16(1) of the Immigration (European Economic Area) Regulations 2016. This will only apply where the right exists under regulation 16(1) because the applicant satisfies the criteria in regulation 16(5) of the 2016 Regulations.

The final, and fifth, description under regulation 4 of the eligibility regulations relates to a person whose only right to reside in the Channel Islands, the Isle of Man or the Republic of Ireland is a right equivalent to one of those mentioned in the second to fourth types of person set out above.

63 Regulation 2(2), eligibility regulations.

64 Regulation 2(2), eligibility regulations.

In relation to the second to fifth descriptions of the types of persons captured by regulation 4, in order to determine whether the only right to reside falls within one of those descriptions, the following is to be disregarded.

(a) A right to reside having been granted where:

   (i) limited leave to enter or remain in the United Kingdom has been granted by virtue of Appendix EU to the immigration rules; or

   (ii) leave to enter the United Kingdom was given by an entry clearance granted under Appendix EU (Family Permit) to the immigration rules.

EEA citizens

The guidance for local authorities at paragraphs 3.9, 3.10, 3.11, 3.19 and 3.22 can assist readers with the position of, and how to deal with applications in relation to, EEA citizens who have established rights under the Agreement on the withdrawal of the United Kingdom of Great Britain and Northern Ireland from the European Union and the European Atomic Energy Community (2019/C 384 I/01)[65] ("the withdrawal agreement"). In short section 7(1) of the Immigration Act 1988 and the Asylum and Immigration Act 1996 have been retained for the purpose of the Housing Act 1996 (and other housing legislation outside the scope of this book) so as to protect the rights of those of EEA citizens and their families which have rights under the withdrawal agreement. As set out at paragraph 3.9 of the guidance for local authorities:

[65] The withdrawal agreement can be accessed at https://www.gov.uk/government/publications/agreement-on-the-withdrawal-of-the-united-kingdom-of-great-britain-and-northern-ireland-from-the-european-union-and-the-european-atomic-energy-communi.

"This will ensure that EEA citizens, and their family members, who:

1. *have acquired limited leave to enter and remain in the UK (also known as pre-settled status) by virtue of Appendix EU of the Immigration Rules ("the EU Settlement Scheme"); or*

2. *were frontier working in the UK prior to 31 December 2020*

will continue to be treated as 'persons not subject to immigration control' in the instances where they would previously have been, so that their eligibility for the allocation of social housing can be judged on the basis of regulation 4 of the Eligibility Regulations as was the case prior to 31 December 2020".

At paragraphs 3.22 to 3.23 of the guidance for local authorities, there is help as to managing applications from EEA citizens from 1 January 2021 and 1 July 2021. The dates result in a difference in treatment. In relation to persons who have moved to the United Kingdom since 1 January 2021, EEA citizens and their family members will (unless they are eligible to apply to the EU Settlement Scheme) come under the new points-based immigration system. The system brings EEA and non-EEA citizens onto the same footing with access to social housing being the same for both types of citizens.

The guidance for local authorities makes it clear where applicants arrive in the United Kingdom after 1 July 2021those EEA citizens who have not applied to the EU Settlement Scheme and/or do not have any other rights to remain lawfully in the United Kingdom will need to either obtain immigration status which would allow them to remain or obtain status under the EU Settlement Scheme.

Decisions on eligibility

Subsections 160ZA(9) and (10) of the Housing Act 1996 provide that a local housing authority shall notify a person of any decision that the person is ineligible for an allocation of housing accommodation. The notice, which shall also set out the local housing authorities grounds for its decision, shall be in writing. If an applicant does not receive the decision, it will be treated as given if the decision was made available for collection (either by the application or by someone on their behalf) at the local authority's offices for a reasonable period of time.

CHAPTER THREE

QUALIFICATION FOR AN ALLOCATION UNDER PART 6 OF THE HOUSING ACT 1996

As set out in Chapter 2, Part 6 of the Housing Act 1996 contains rules for the allocation of accommodation by local housing authorities to those persons that are eligible and/or qualify for such an allocation. This chapter takes a looks at how a person can qualify for an allocation of housing accommodation.

Generally, it is good practice for a local housing authority to consider qualification onto its scheme both at the time of the application for housing and at the time when an allocation might be made.[66]

Who can qualify for an allocation of housing?

Subject to the eligibility provisions discussed in Chapter 2, there is a relatively broad discretion for local housing authorities in England who may allocate housing accommodation to a person (whether via that person's application or otherwise) if that person is someone who, or on a joint application at least one of the applicants is someone who, qualifies under the local housing authority's criteria.[67] This will be subject to any

66 See paragraph 3.32 of the *Allocation of accommodation: guidance for local authorities*, updated 15 May 2023, which also sets out that this is particularly important if there is a long period of time between the initial application and an allocation.

67 Subsections 160ZA(6) and (7), Housing Act 1996.

regulations made by the Secretary of State under subsection 160ZA(8) of the Housing Act 1996.

The Secretary of State has used the powers under section 160ZA and made the following regulations which will need to be taken into account when a local housing authority sets its qualification criteria.

- Allocation of Housing (Qualification Criteria for Armed Forces) (England) Regulations 2012/1869.
- Allocation of Housing (Qualification Criteria for Right to Move) (England) Regulations 2015/967.

Armed forces

The Allocation of Housing (Qualification Criteria for Armed Forces) (England) Regulations 2012 ("Armed Forces Regulations 2012") came into force on 24 August 2012 and provide that local housing authorities must not use local connection (within the meaning of section 199 of the Housing Act 1996) as a qualifying criteria in certain circumstances concerning the armed forces.

The Armed Forces Regulations 2012 adopt the same definitions for regular and reserve forces. These definitions are found in section 374 of the Armed Forces Act 2006 which sets out:

(a) "regular forces" means the Royal Navy, the Royal Marines, the regular army or the Royal Air Force; and,

(b) "reserve forces" means the Royal Fleet Reserve, the Royal Naval Reserve, the Royal Marines Reserve, the Regular Reserve, the Army Reserve, the Royal Air Force Reserve or the Royal Auxiliary Air Force.

Under regulation 3 of the Armed Forces Regulations 2012, a local housing authority may not use the criterion that *"a relevant person must have a local connection to the district of a local housing authority"* when deciding classes of persons who would not be qualifying persons under section 160ZA(7) of the Housing Act 1996. A relevant person for the purpose of this regulation is a person who:

> *"(a) is serving in the regular forces or who has served in the regular forces within five years of the date of their application for an allocation of housing under Part 6 of the 1996 Act;*
>
> *(b) has recently ceased, or will cease to be entitled, to reside in accommodation provided by the Ministry of Defence following the death of that person's spouse or civil partner where—*
>
> > *(i) the spouse or civil partner has served in the regular forces; and*
> >
> > *(ii) their death was attributable (wholly or partly) to that service; or*
>
> *(c) is serving or has served in the reserve forces and who is suffering from a serious injury, illness or disability which is attributable (wholly or partly) to that service".*[68]

So, a local housing authority must not apply local connection criterion to:

(a) persons that are serving in the regular armed forces or has so served in the five years before their application for housing;

(b) spouses or civil partners who have to leave armed forces accommodation following the death or their spouse or partner where the death can be in some way attributed to their service in the armed forces; or,

68 See reg. 3(3) of the armed forces regulations 2012.

(c) persons who are suffering from a serious injury, illness or disability and are members, or were members, of the reserve armed forces where such illness, injury or disability is in some way is attributable to their service in the armed forces.

In June 2020, the Secretary of State for Housing, Communities and Local Government published statutory guidance under section 169, Housing Act 1996 in relation to the Armed Forces: *Improving access to social housing for members of the Armed Forces.*[69] The guidance has a section dealing with qualification and repeats what can be found in the Armed Forces Regulations 2012.[70] The guidance reminds us of the special position of members of the Armed Forces (including bereaved spouses and civil partners and reservists) whose employment requires them to travel and may result in serious injury requiring access to treatment, care and support in a certain area. In terms of travelling and deployment as a part of their employment, this means that certain members of the Armed Forces are less likely to be able to establish links with any particular local authority area. As such, there is likely to be a clear disadvantage caused to them by any local connection requirements within allocations schemes.

The guidance, however, goes further than the Armed Forces Regulations 2012 in relation to qualification. It recognises that family circumstances can change in the Armed Forces community and "strongly encourages" local authorities not to apply any local connection requirements to those who are divorced or separated spouses or civil partners of service personnel who need to move out of accommodation provided by the

[69] https://www.gov.uk/government/publications/improving-access-to-social-housing-for-members-of-the-armed-forces/improving-access-to-social-housing-for-members-of-the-armed-forces.

[70] See paragraphs 12 to 15 of the Statutory guidance, *Improving access to social housing for members of the Armed Forces,* Secretary of State for Housing, Communities and Local Government, 27 June 2020.

Ministry of Defence.[71] The guidance also reminds local authorities that they do retain a discretion where there are exceptional circumstances and encourages them to think about disadvantage to the Armed Forces community in relation to all other qualification criteria adopted.[72] As to other criteria often used by local housing authorities, one example used in the guidance is where local authorities make reference to an applicant's income or assists in relation to qualification. It is suggested that a local housing authority would be able to disregard any lump sum received by a member of the armed forces as compensation for an injury or disability sustained on active service.[73] This is a sensible suggestion as it would be a harsh result if such compensation meant a person who is or was a member of the armed forces did not qualify for an allocation of accommodation.

The right to move

In England, local connection may not be used by a local housing authority in deciding whether a "relevant person" qualifies for an allocation if the allocation involves a transfer of housing accommodation for that person from the district of another local housing authority in England.[74] This has applied since 20 April 2015. A relevant person is a person who:

---

71 See paragraphs 16 to 18 of the Statutory guidance, *Improving access to social housing for members of the Armed Forces,* Secretary of State for Housing, Communities and Local Government, 27 June 2020.

72 See paragraph 19 of the Statutory guidance, *Improving access to social housing for members of the Armed Forces,* Secretary of State for Housing, Communities and Local Government, 27 June 2020.

73 See paragraphs 20 to 20 of the Statutory guidance, *Improving access to social housing for members of the Armed Forces,* Secretary of State for Housing, Communities and Local Government, 27 June 2020.

74 Regulation 3 of the Allocation of Housing (Qualification Criteria for Right to Move) (England) Regulations 2015/967.

(a) falls within section 159(4A)(a) or (b) of the Housing Act 1996 *i.e.* a person who is already a secure or introductory tenant, or an assured tenant of housing accommodation held by a PRPSH or a RSL (see Chapter 1);

(b) is to be given reasonable preference under section 166A(3)(e) *i.e.* a person who needs to move to a particular locality in the district of the authority, where failure to meet that need would cause hardship (to themselves or to others) (see Chapter 4); and

(c) has a need to move for work *i.e.* the person works in the district of the local housing authority, or has been offered work in the district of the local housing authority, and the authority is satisfied that the person has a genuine intention of taking up the offer of work. The person will not have a need to move if the work or the offer of work is:

- of a short-term or marginal nature;
- ancillary to work carried out in another district; or
- voluntary work *i.e.* where no payment is received or the only payment due to be made is a payment in respect of any expenses reasonably incurred by the relevant person in the course of being engaged in such work.[75]

Alongside the Allocation of Housing (Qualification Criteria for Right to Move) (England) Regulations 2015 ("Right to Move Regulations 2015"), the Secretary of State for Communities and Local Government issued statutory guidance under section 169 of the Housing Act 1996 on 27 March 2015. The Right to Move and social housing allocations

[75] Regulations 4 and 5 of the Allocation of Housing (Qualification Criteria for Right to Move) (England) Regulations 2015/967.

guidance considers qualification at paragraphs 11 to 34. It is especially useful to local housing authorities in giving guidance, at paragraphs 20 to 27, as the meanings of the different types of work that mean a person does not have a need to move under the Right to Move Regulations 2015. The guidance also makes clear that the term "work" under the Right to Move Regulations 2015 includes an apprenticeship[76] and the type of evidence that might be required to prove a job offer is genuine and/or there is a genuine intention to take up an offer of work.[77]

Setting qualification criteria

The Court of Appeal has held that the qualification criteria that a local housing authority can set in accordance with section 160ZA is subject to the reasonable preference duty. In *R (on the application of Jakimaviciute) v Hammersmith and Fulham LBC* [2014] EWCA Civ 1438; [2015] 3 ALL ER 490, it was held at [28] to [31] that whilst a local housing authority's power to decide what classes of person qualify under section 160ZA(7) was discretionary and made no reference to being subject to the reasonable preference duty in section 166A(3). Reading Part 6 as a whole, a close relationship between section 160ZA(7) and the reasonable preference duty in section 166A(3) can be seen.

> *"On the natural interpretation of the statutory provisions, the setting of the qualification criteria was subject to the reasonable preference duty."*[78]

---

[76] See paragraph 28 of Right to Move and social housing allocations, Secretary of State for Housing, Communities and Local Government, 27 March 2015.

[77] See paragraphs 29 to 34 of Right to Move and social housing allocations, Secretary of State for Housing, Communities and Local Government, 27 March 2015.

[78] *R (on the application of Jakimaviciute) v Hammersmith and Fulham LBC* [2014] EWCA Civ 1438; [2015] 3 ALL ER 490 at [31].

Reasonable preference will be discussed in more detail in Chapter 4 but *Jakimaviciute* confirmed that a person who has a reasonable preference under an allocation scheme can be excluded by the setting of qualification criteria. Prior to *Jakimaviciute,* the case of *R v Wolverhampton MBC ex p. Watters* [1997] 3 F.C.R. 747, held that even though an applicant fell within a reasonable preference category, a local authority could refuse to allocate housing where that person was in substantial rent arrears. The guidance for local authorities, which is discussed next below, also considers the type of qualification criteria which may result in a person being excluded even though they have a reasonable preference.

Jakimaviciute also confirmed, however, that a local housing authority cannot use qualification criteria so as to disqualify the majority of people owed a duty in a particular category of person.[79] In that case, Hammersmith and Fulham LBC were operating an allocation scheme which at paragraph 2.14(d) set out that the following class of persons would not normally qualify for registration under their scheme:

> *"Homeless applicants placed in long term suitable temporary accommodation under the main homelessness duty, unless the property does not meet the needs of the household or is about to be ended through no fault of the applicant. Long term temporary accommodation can include private sector homes let via the council or a housing association under a leasing arrangement, and non-secure tenancies on regeneration estates."*[80]

This was the paragraph under challenge. The Court held at [47]:

> *"... The disqualification effected by para.2.14(d) is fundamentally at odds with the requirement under s.166A(3)(b) to frame a scheme so as*

---

79 *R (on the application of Jakimaviciute) v Hammersmith and Fulham LBC* [2014] EWCA Civ 1438; [2015] 3 ALL ER 490 at [47].

80 *R (on the application of Jakimaviciute) v Hammersmith and Fulham LBC* [2014] EWCA Civ 1438; [2015] 3 ALL ER 490 at [2].

to secure that reasonable preference is given to people who are owed a housing duty under one of the provisions of Pt 7. The great majority of people within that class, far from being given any preference, are excluded altogether from consideration for housing accommodation under the Scheme; and they are excluded for a reason that cannot sit with Parliament's decision to define the s.166A(3)(b) class as it did... It is the exclusion of a large proportion of one of those classes that causes the problem…".

There have also been some more recent cases dealing with these issues. In *R (Montero) v Lewisham LBC* [2021] EWHC 1359; [2021] PTSR 1725, Lewisham's allocation scheme provided:

"2.2 Disqualification from the housing list or from receiving an offer

As a result of the severe shortage of housing in Lewisham, we have identified certain groups of applicants to whom we will not normally allocate housing. Such applicants are either disqualified from being on the housing list or are disqualified from receiving an offer (although they are allowed to be on the housing list). The Council considers that the factors set out in the grounds for disqualification below will ordinarily outweigh any reasonable preference to which an applicant is entitled.

The effect of being disqualified from the housing list is that your application will be cancelled. During the period of disqualification you will be unable to reapply. When the period of disqualification comes to an end, if you wish to pursue your application again, you will have to reapply. Your application will be taken to have been made on the date of your reapplication."[81]

81 *R (Montero) v Lewisham LBC* [2021] EWHC 1359; [2021] PTSR 1725 at [16].

Section 2.2. of Lewisham's allocation policy then went onto set out circumstances which could result in a person being disqualified. Section 2.2.2 of the allocation policy dealt with local connection. There were a number of exceptions but generally, for the purpose of the allocation policy, local connection meant:

> "You are currently resident in Lewisham and have been resident for a period of 5 years".[82]

The Court held that Lewisham's allocation policy was lawful. Henshaw J held it was lawful to adopt a rule which excluded individual applicants by reference to factors of general application, such as lack of local connection, and such a rule *"does not fundamentally cut across the relevant reasonable preference category".*[83] Lewisham's policy was not one that sort to exclude an entire class (or the majority of a class) that should be given reasonable preference.

In *Khayyat v Westminster City Council* [2023] EWHC 30 (Admin); [2023] HLR 23, the Court held, citing *Jakimaviciute,* that:

> *"...An exclusion by reference to a factor of general application is not a redefinition of the statutory scheme. All those in each of the statutory reasonable preference categories will have the potential to be given the relevant reasonable preference. The fact that there is an additional qualification and a potential exclusion which applies across all the categories does not affect that... By way of contrast an exclusion by reference to a factor which is not of general application will inevitably amount to a redefinition of the statutory scheme. That is because it will exclude from the provision of reasonable preference members of the category or categories to whom the factor applies notwithstanding the*

82 *R (Montero) v Lewisham LBC* [2021] EWHC 1359; [2021] PTSR 1725 at [18].

83 *R (Montero) v Lewisham LBC* [2021] EWHC 1359; [2021] PTSR 1725 at [68].

fact that the Act provides that persons in that category or categories should receive reasonable preference".[84]

In that case, *Westminster's* allocation scheme was held to be unlawful as it operated so as *"to exclude persons from receipt of a reasonable preference by reference to factors other than factors of general application".*[85] Westminster's scheme excluded homeless persons to whom the so-called "main housing duty"[86] was not owed.

Local housing authorities have to be careful when framing their allocations schemes, therefore, that the effect of any qualification criterion is not to exclude the majority of a class of persons from that scheme. If it does so, it is likely to be found to be unlawful. Such an approach is not the same, however, as excluding individuals by reference to certain factors which could be applied to all applicants, for example, anti-social behaviour or rent arrears.

The guidance for local authorities

Local housing authorities should take into account the statutory guidance for local authorities when considering what qualification criteria would be appropriate. Qualification is dealt with in chapter 3 of the guidance for local authorities at paragraphs 3.24 to 3.37.

The guidance at 3.27 suggests, by way of an example, that local housing authorities may wish to disqualify those who have a reasonable preference under the scheme for reasons of anti-social behaviour. This is something that will often be seen in allocation schemes and is usually linked to the wording dealing with anti-social behaviour in Part 1 of the Anti-Social

---

84 Khayyat v Westminster City Council [2023] EWHC 30 (Admin); [2023] HLR 23 at [58].

85 Khayyat v Westminster City Council [2023] EWHC 30 (Admin); [2023] HLR 23 at [61].

86 This is the duty under section 193 of the Housing Act 1996.

Behaviour, Crime and Policing Act 2014 (*i.e.* the basis upon which a court may grant an injunction against a person) or in ground 2 of schedule 2 to the Housing Act 1985 (which is a ground for possession based upon behaviour).

The guidance for local authorities also urges local housing authorities to think about the position of those fleeing domestic abuse when setting qualification criteria. In any event, in respect of domestic abuse, regard should also be had to the statutory guidance – *Improving access to social housing for victims of domestic abuse* ("domestic abuse guidance") – that was published on 10 November 2018 and last updated on 25 January 2022.[87] The guidance was issued under section 169 of the Housing Act 1996. Qualification for social housing is dealt with at paragraphs 16 to 21 of the domestic abuse guidance.

Importantly, it recognises that when someone is seeking to remove themselves and their family away from domestic abuse it could be necessary for their safety for them to travel to different areas to seek assistance. Whilst the domestic abuse guidance makes reference to the updated Homelessness Code of Guidance, it also directs local authorities to the statutory guidance – *Providing social housing for local people* – which was published on 31 December 2013. This guidance was issued under section 169 of the Housing Act 1996 and is also referred to as "the local connections guidance". In the local connections guidance, local housing authorities are encouraged to include a residency requirement as part of their qualification criteria of at least two years but there is a reminder of the need to think about exceptions to that criteria over and above those dealt with by way of regulations (as above). An area ripe for such an exception, and often seen within allocation schemes, is where someone is fleeing domestic abuse and finds themselves applying for housing at a

[87] The domestic abuse guidance can be accessed at: https://www.gov.uk/government/publications/improving-access-to-social-housing-for-victims-of-domestic- abuse/improving-access-to-social-housing-for-victims-of-domestic-abuse.

local authority in an area with which they have little or no connection; they often do not have a connection which would satisfy any residency criteria. Such an exception is actively encouraged in the domestic abuse guidance and the guidance for local authorities.[88]

The guidance for local authorities discourages allocating social housing to those who own their own homes although it recognises there may be exceptional circumstances that warrant such an allocation. The example given in the guidance as to such an exceptional circumstances is where elderly owner occupiers need to move into sheltered accommodation for care and support.[89]

Finally, the guidance for local authorities:

(a) notes that there may be *"sound policy reasons"* for treating existing tenants and new applicants differently in the setting of qualification criteria; and,

(b) reminds local housing authorities of the need to maintain a discretion so, where there are exceptional circumstances, qualification criteria can be disapplied.

Where a local authority maintains a discretion, as it should, for exceptional circumstances, it must be clear as to how this should operate in practice. I do not mean that there should be a fetter on any discretion; I mean that those dealing with housing applications should be alive to the fact there is such a discretion within their scheme and be ready to exercise the same when circumstances warrant it.

---

88 See paragraph 19 of *Improving access to social housing for victims of domestic abuse*, updated 25 January 2022 and paragraph 3.28 of the *Allocation of accommodation: guidance for local authorities*, updated 15 May 2023.

89 See paragraph 3.29 of the *Allocation of accommodation: guidance for local authorities*, updated 15 May 2023.

Other relevant statutory considerations when setting qualification criteria

Referred to in the guidance for local authorities as the "equalities legislation", local housing authorities do need to take into account of their duties under the Equality Act 2010 when setting qualification criteria.[90] They also need to take into account the requirement to give reasonable preference (see chapter 4).

A number of cases have highlighted that allocation schemes that directly or indirectly discriminate against someone contrary to the provisions within the Equality Act 2010 can be challenged and may well be found to be unlawful.

By way of example, in *R (Ward) v Hillingdon; R (Gullu) v Hillingdon* [2019] EWCA Civ 692; [2019] P.T.S.R. 1738, Hillingdon's allocation scheme provided that persons who could not show 10 years continuous residence in the district would be disqualified from joining the scheme. Ms Ward was an Irish traveller who lived a nomadic lifestyle. Mr Gullu was a Kurdish refugee who had not been in the country ten years. The Court of Appeal found the policy was indirectly discriminatory as it disadvantaged travellers and non-UK nationals compared to persons without those characteristics. Hillingdon, therefore, needed to justify the

---

[90] Whilst not statutory guidance under the Housing Act 1996, the Equality and Human Rights Commission has issued Housing and disabled people: a toolkit for local authorities in England which can be accessed at: https://www.equalityhumanrights.com/en/publication-download/housing-and-disabled-people-toolkit-local- authorities-england). In addition, it is also worth readers having a look at *Providing social housing for local people: statutory guidance on social housing allocations for local authorities in England: Equality statement*, April 2014. The equality statement can be accessed at: https://assets.publishing.service.gov.uk/government/uploads/system/uploads/attachment_data/file/303579/140401_providing_social_housing_for_local_people_-_sor_-_equality_impact.pdf.

discrimination under section 19 of the Equality Act 2010 but had not done so (although it would be open to them to do so at later stage).

Another example is *R (HA) v Ealing* [2015] EWHC 2375 (Admin); [2018] HLR 2, CA. In that case, Ealing had a 5-year requirement for local residence. HA had fled domestic abuse with her children and come to Ealing. It was held that the scheme was indirectly discriminatory for lack of justification, amongst other issues.

Any local authority when framing an allocations scheme will need to carry out assessments under the Equality Act 2010 where necessary. Such assessments do not have to be included within the allocation scheme itself although the authority will want to highlight the Equality Act 2010 has been taken into account somewhere within its scheme.

Decisions on qualification

As with decisions on eligibility, it is subsections 160ZA(9) and (10) of the Housing Act 1996 that provide for notification by a local authority of any decision that the person does not qualify for an allocation of housing accommodation. The notice, which shall also set out the local housing authorities grounds for its decision, shall be in writing. If an applicant does not receive the decision, it will be treated as given if the decision was made available for collection (either by the application or by someone on their behalf) at the local authority's offices for a reasonable period of time.

Consequences of a negative decision on qualification

A negative decision by a local housing authority which concludes that an applicant should not be treated as a qualifying person is not the end of the line. Where an applicant thinks they should have been treated as a qualifying person, they can make a fresh application to the local housing authority for an allocation of housing accommodation.[91]

---

[91] Subsection 160ZA(11), Housing Act 1996.

CHAPTER FOUR

REASONABLE AND ADDITIONAL PREFERENCE

Reasonable and additional preference are two key features of housing allocation and how a local housing authority should prioritise applicants and shape their allocations scheme. This chapter considers the classes of persons to which reasonable or additional preference should be given and where the exceptions lie. Section 166A of the Housing Act 1996 is the main section that readers should consider alongside Chapter 4 of the Allocation of accommodation: guidance for local authorities ("statutory guidance for local authorities").

Reasonable preference and framing the scheme

Under section 166A(3) of the Housing Act 1996 there is a requirement that allocation scheme must be framed to ensure reasonable preference is given to a number of different categories of applicant. Reasonable preference *"requires that positive favour should be shown to applications which satisfy any of the relevant criteria. To use colloquial language they should be given a reasonable head start"*.[92]

The effect of the statutory framework is that the scheme, once established, must be followed; the scheme will decide which applicant is

[92] *R v Wolverhampton MBC ex p Watters* (1997) 29 HLR 931 CA, at 938 *per* Judge LJ. This case dealt with the previous provisions under section 22 of the Housing Act 1985 but has been cited in relation to the Housing Act 1996 in *R (A) v Lambeth LBC; R (Lindsay) v Lambeth LBC* [2002] EWCA Civ 1084; [2002] HLR 57, CA at [15].

selected for a property, and where on the waiting list an applicant would be.[93]

It is noted at paragraph 4.5 of the statutory guidance for local authorities that a local authority will need to be able to show its scheme overall has been developed with *"reasonable preference ... given to all"* of the reasonable preference categories despite the lack of any requirement to give equal weight to the each of categories. This does not mean, however, that cumulative preference has to be given. In *R (oao of Ahmad) v Newham LBC* [2009] UKHL 14; [2009] PTSR 632, there was a challenge to Newham's allocation scheme which was said to be unlawful because, amongst other things, it failed to take into account the cumulative needs of a family. Newham lost in the High Court and the Court of Appeal – *i.e.* both courts decided that the allocation scheme was unlawful – but the House of Lords (as it then was) allowed Newham's appeal. The allocations scheme was not unlawful.

The Court held, amongst other things, that the scheme complied with the express statutory requirements (*i.e.* it gave reasonable preferences to the defined categories of persons) and there was no statutory requirement to determine priorities between those people who fell within a reasonable preference category (*i.e.* there was no need to give cumulative preference).[94]

At the time of the *Ahmad* challenge, it was section 167 of the Housing Act 1996 that set out reasonable preference categories but the conclusions of the Court must apply to allocation schemes that are framed in accordance with section 166A(3). This is supported by the citation, reliance and approval of *Ahmad* in cases dealing with the operation of

93 *R (Flores) v Southwark* [2020] EWCA Civ 1697; [2021] HLR 16.

94 *R (oao of Ahmad) v Newham LBC* [2009] UKHL 14; [2009] PTSR 632 at [1], [2], [8], [10], [37]-38] and [49]. See also the statutory guidance for local authorities at paragraph 4.5.

section 166A(3)[95] as well as the inclusion of the case in the statutory guidance for local authorities at paragraphs 4.5.

Categories of persons to be given reasonable preference

The first category is people who are homeless within the meaning of Part 7 of the Housing Act 1996. Part 7 of the Housing Act 1996 is outside the scope of this book but, in brief, a person is homeless if they have no accommodation available for their occupation which they:

- are entitled to occupy because of an interest in the accommodation or because of a court order;

- have a licence to occupy the accommodation (the licence can be express which generally means it will be clear on the face of an agreement in writing or implied *e.g.* a licence can be implied through the conduct of the parties); or

- occupy the accommodation under an enactment or rule of law which allows them to remain in occupation or restricts the rights of another person to obtain possession that accommodation. [96]

The accommodation also has to be reasonable to continue to occupy. If it is not, a person is not treated as having accommodation.[97] The phrase "reasonable to continue to occupy" is not exhaustively defined within Part 7 of the Housing Act 1996 and, when considering this question,

---

95 See, for example, *R (Alemi) v Westminster City Council* [2015] PTSR 1339 at [3] and *R (XC) v Southwark LBC* [2017] EWHC 736 (Admin); [2017] HLR 24 at [93].

96 Subsections 175(1)(a)-(c), Housing Act 1996. Readers can also have a look at the *Homelessness code of guidance for local authorities* which was last updated on 27 October 2023 (chapter 6 in particular deals with those that are homeless or threatened with homelessness).

97 Subsections 175(3), Housing Act 1996.

regard can be had to the *"general circumstances prevailing in the relation to housing in the district of the local housing authority"* to which a homelessness application has been made.[98] In addition, subsection 177(1) of the Housing Act 1996 makes it clear that accommodation will not be reasonable to continue to occupy *"if it is probable that this will lead to violence or domestic abuse against him, or against (a) a person who normally resides with him as a member of his family, or (b) any other person who might reasonably be expected to reside with him"*. The Secretary of State may also make orders in relation to the question of whether accommodation is reasonable to continue to occupy.[99]

A person will also be homeless if they have accommodation but they cannot secure entry to it or it consists of a moveable structure and there is no place where they are entitled or permitted to place it and to reside in it.[100]

The second category – also linked to a local housing authority's homelessness duties – is people who are owed a duty by any local housing authority under a number of sections of the Part 7 of the Housing Act 1996 (or under sections 65(2) or 68(2) of the Housing Act 1985[101]). The sections under Part 7 are:

- section 190(2) – duties to persons becoming intentionally homeless;

---

98 Subsection 177(2), Housing Act 1996.

99 Subsection 177(3) and see the Homelessness (Suitability of Accommodation) Order 1996 (SI No. 3204).

100 Subsection 175(2)(a)-(c), Housing Act 1996.

101 Sections 65(2) (duties to persons found to be homeless) and 68(2) (duties to persons whose applications are referred) of the Housing Act 1985 were repealed when Part 7 of the Housing Act 1996 came into force (from 20 January 1997) but are still set out, albeit in brackets, in section 166A(3) of the Housing Act 1996.

- section 193(2) – duty to persons with priority need who are not intentionally homeless *i.e.* the so-called "main housing duty"; and,

- section 195(2) – duties in cases of threatened homelessness.

The second category also includes those who are occupying accommodation provided by an authority under the main housing duty in section 192(3) of the Housing Act 1996.[102]

The first two categories of applicant set out above do not include people who are to be disregarded because they would only have fallen into either category because the local housing authority had regard to a restricted person within the meaning of Part 7 of the Housing Act 1996.[103] "Restricted person" is defined in section 184(7) of the Housing Act 1996 and means a person that is not eligible for Part 7 assistance who is subject to immigration control[104] and does not have leave to enter or remain in the United Kingdom or does have leave to enter or remain but that leave is conditional on not having recourse to public funds.

The next three categories of applicant in section 166A(3) to which reasonable preference must be given are:

- people living in insanitary or overcrowded housing or otherwise residing in unsatisfactory housing conditions;

- people who need to move on medical or welfare grounds (including any grounds relating to a disability); and,

---

102 Subsections 166A(3)(a)-(b) of the Housing Act 1996.

103 Subsection 166A(4) of the Housing Act 1996.

104 Within the meaning of the Asylum and Immigration Act 1996.

- people who need to move to a particular locality in the district of the authority, where failure to meet that need would cause hardship to themselves or to others (this could include, but is not limited to, the need to continue with, or take up, particular training, education or employment).[105]

In relation to overcrowding, as a minimum, it is recommended the "bedroom standard" is used by local housing authorities as the measure. This recommendation is set out at paragraph 4.8 of the statutory guidance for local authorities and provides as follows.

"The bedroom standard allocates a separate bedroom to each:

- *married or cohabiting couple*
- *adult aged 21 years or more*
- *pair of adolescents aged 10-20 years of the same sex*
- *pair of children aged under 10 years regardless of sex".*

Whilst it is a matter for the local housing authority and not an exhaustive list, Annex 1 of the statutory guidance for local authorities also sets out examples of those things which are likely to be indicators of the criteria in the insanitary, overcrowded and unsatisfactory housing conditions reasonable preference category. They are as follows.

"Insanitary, overcrowded and unsatisfactory housing conditions

- *lacking bathroom or kitchen*

105 Subsections 166A(c)-(e) of the Housing Act 1996 and the statutory guidance for local authorities at paragraph 4.11 (hardship grounds).

- *lacking inside WC*
- *lacking cold or hot water supplies, electricity, gas, or adequate heating*
- *lack of access to a garden for young children*
- *sharing living room, kitchen, bathroom/WC*
- *property in disrepair*
- *poor internal or external arrangements*
- *young children in flats above ground floor".*

Authorities will need to consider carefully what is included in medical or welfare grounds; the category is broad. At paragraphs 4.9 and 4.10 of the statutory guidance for local authorities, guidance is given on what the categories can encompass and this includes people:

- who need to move because of access needs;
- who need to move because of a disability;
- with learning disabilities (including those who wish to live independently but need care and support to do so);
- with physical disabilities;
- who need stability in their life due to their circumstances *e.g.* care leavers or those who have embarked on a programme to help them combat addiction; and,

- who provide or receive care and support *e.g.* foster carers and those who care for a child where the parents are no longer able.

Further Annex 1, in the same way as it sets out some indicators in relation to insanitary, overcrowded and unsatisfactory housing conditions, produces a list of matters which are examples of indicators for the medical or welfare grounds reasonable preference category to assist local housing authorities. There are fifteen indicators set out and they include: chronic or progressive medical conditions, infirmity due to old age, the need to recover from emotional or sexual abuse, young people at risk, the need for improved heating (on medical grounds) and the need to be near friends/relatives or medical facility on medical grounds.

In addition, there is other statutory guidance relevant to the preference categories.

- *"Improving access to social housing for victims of domestic abuse"*[106] at paragraphs 30 to 33 *"strongly encourages"* local housing authorities *"to apply the medical and welfare reasonable preference category to victims and their families who have escaped abuse and are being accommodated in a refuge or other temporary accommodation"*. If it was not obvious, the guidance makes it clear that those recovering from the impact of domestic abuse are likely to have medical and welfare needs.

- *"Improving access to social housing for members of the Armed Forces"*[107] at paragraphs 26 to 34 considers the mental health and

---

106 Last updated on 25 January 2022 and available here: https://www.gov.uk/government/publications/improving-access-to-social-housing-for-victims-of-domestic-abuse/improving-access-to-social-housing-for-victims-of-domestic-abuse.

107 Published on 27 June 2020 and available here: https://www.gov.uk/government/publications/improving-access-to-social-

wellbeing of the armed forces and goes further than Annex 1 and sets out that the reasonable preference category *"in the Government's view...would encompass anyone who needs to move as a result of a mental ill health conditions"*. In setting out that local authorities need to be sensitive to such issues and not have an onerous evidential burden, the guidance goes on to highlight certain conditions that impact upon those in the armed forces: depression, anxiety and Post Traumatic Stress Disorder.

Excluding those with reasonable preference from qualification under a scheme

Despite the broad discretion authorities have in the allocation of housing, a local housing authority needs to be careful not to adopt an allocations policy that excludes a large number of people who would be entitled to receive a reasonable preference. In *R (oao Jakimaviciute) v Hammersmith and Fulham LBC* [2014] EWCA Civ 1438; [2015] 3 All ER 490, Richards LJ summarised the position at [47] where he said he did not accept there was a power to exclude a large proportion of those who fall into a class that should be given a reasonable preference. He did not accept such an exclusion was inherent in the flexibility allowed to an authority in securing that reasonable preference is given.

There is a difference, however, between an individual applicant being excluded from qualification under an local housing authority's scheme because of a rule in the scheme by reference to factors of general application, for example, if someone is in rent arrears or does not have a local connection compared to wholesale disqualification of a class of person who should be given reasonable preference.[108] A person can, therefore, be disqualified in a reasonable preference category; reasonable

housing-for-members-of-the-armed-forces/improving-access-to-social-housing-for-members-of-the-armed-forces#priority-for-social-housing.

108 See *e.g. R (Alemi) v Westminster City Council* [2015] PTSR 1339 and *R (Montero) v Lewisham LBC* [2021] EWHC 13925; [2021] PTSR 1725.

preference does not mean that every person who falls within such a class has to be given priority over every person not within such a class.

The above approach was confirmed more recently in *Khayyat v Westminster City Council* [2023] EWHC 30 (Admin); [2023] H.L.R. 23, where Eyre J set out at [35]:

> *"It follows that a local housing authority can adopt a policy which excludes individuals who would otherwise be entitled to receive a reasonable preference (and so to be placed on a housing register) provided it does so by way of "factors of general application". That is by way of factors which are capable of applying to an individual in any of the section 166A(3) categories (thus a person in any of those categories may be in rent arrears or may have or may lack a local connection)".*

A local housing authority cannot, however, give no preference and remove altogether the *"potential of being allocated social housing"* from an applicant who should be afforded a reasonable preference.[109]

Additional preference

Unlike a scheme having to give priority to certain categories of people afforded reasonable preference, an allocations scheme *may* also give additional preference to particular descriptions of people with urgent housing needs *i.e.* people falling within one or more of the categories to

---

[109] *R (Alemi) v Westminster City Council* [2015] EWHC 1765 (Admin); [2015] PTSR 1339 at [28]-[33]. In *Alemi,* the allocation scheme was held to be unlawful and in breach of section 166A(3) of the Housing Act 1996 in circumstances where it suspended an applicant's ability to bid for social housing until twelve months had passed following the acceptance of the main housing duty under section 193(2) of the Housing Act by the authority.

which reasonable preference should be given.[110] This means a local housing authority has a discretion to provide "additional preference" for certain persons if they are in urgent housing need.

The statutory guidance for local authorities gives three examples of the type of persons it says local housing authorities should consider giving additional preference to. The examples are:

- "those who need to move urgently because of a life threatening illness or sudden disability
- families in severe overcrowding which poses a serious health hazard
- those who are homeless and require urgent re-housing as a result of violence or threats of violence, including intimidated witnesses, and those escaping serious anti-social behaviour or domestic violence".[111]

The scheme must, however, be framed so as to give additional preference to a person with urgent housing needs who falls within one or more of the categories of person to whom reasonable preference must be given to and who:

> *"(i) is serving in the regular forces and is suffering from a serious injury, illness or disability which is attributable (wholly or partly) to the person's service,*

[110] Section 166A(3), Housing Act 1996.

[111] Allocation of accommodation: guidance for local authorities (https://www.gov.uk/guidance/allocation-of-accommodation-guidance-for-local-authorities/chapter-4-framing-an-allocation-scheme) at paragraph 4.13.

(ii) formerly served in the regular forces,

(iii) has recently ceased, or will cease to be entitled, to reside in accommodation provided by the Ministry of Defence following the death of that person's spouse or civil partner who has served in the regular forces and whose death was attributable (wholly or partly) to that service, or

(iv) is serving or has served in the reserve forces and is suffering from a serious injury, illness or disability which is attributable (wholly or partly) to the person's service".[112]

The above provision was added into section 166A(3) by the Housing Act 1996 (Additional Preference for Armed Forces) (England) Regulations 2012.[113] As set out in Chapter 3 dealing with qualification, "the regular forces" and "the reserve forces" as used within subsection 166A(3) have the same meaning as set out in section 374 of the Armed Forces Act 2006 *i.e.*

(c) "regular forces" means the Royal Navy, the Royal Marines, the regular army or the Royal Air Force; and,

(d) "reserve forces" means the Royal Fleet Reserve, the Royal Naval Reserve, the Royal Marines Reserve, the Regular Reserve, the Army Reserve, the Royal Air Force Reserve or the Royal Auxiliary Air Force.

As well as considering mental health and wellbeing in relation to the armed forces (as set out above), the statutory guidance *"Improving access to social housing for members of the Armed Forces"* also has sections dealing

---

112 Subsections 166A(3)(i)-(iv), Housing Act 1996. See also Chapter 3 for a discussion on the armed forces when it comes to qualification for a Part 6 allocation.

113 SI No. 2989.

with priority for social housing (see paragraphs 22 to 25) and allocation flexibilities[114] (see paragraphs 35 to 37). The guidance repeats what is set out in subsection 166A(3) and makes it clear that an "illness or disability" for the purpose of additional preference would include a relevant mental condition.

Amendments to subsection 166A(3)

The Secretary of State may introduce regulations so as to amend or repeal any part of subsection 166A(3) or to identify additional descriptions of those to who a preference should be given.[115] The Secretary of State can also bring in regulations that tell local housing authorities what factors must not be taken into account when allocating housing accommodation.[116]

Determining priorities

Under subsection 166A(5) of the Housing Act 1996, there is a further discretion given to local housing authorities. Under the subsection, an allocation scheme may also set out how it determines priorities for the allocation of housing accommodation to those who fall within subsection 166A(3) as discussed above. In *R (Alemi) v Westminster City Council* [2015] EWHC 1765 (Admin); [2015] PTSR 1339 it was explained at [29] that:

> *"the examples…in section 166A(5)…reflect the legislative intention to recognise features of the circumstances of applicants for whom, as a sub-group, [a local housing authority] may justify a differentiation in the priority they are given within a larger group which must be given a reasonable preference in the allocation of social housing… What those*

114 This section is also relevant to the determination of priorities which is discussed below.

115 Subsection 166A(7), Housing Act 1996.

116 Subsection 166A(8), Housing Act 1996.

> *examples in section 166A(5) do not do is to altogether remove them from the potential of being allocated social housing. In a time where there is a paucity of social housing it may be an entirely theoretical potential, but it is none the less a potential".*

The "examples" in subsection 166A(5) referred to in *Alemi* are the number of factors set out which may be used within a scheme to prioritise an allocation. These are:

(a) the applicant's financial resources which they are able to use to meet housing costs;

(b) an applicant's behaviour (or the behaviour of another member of the household) and their suitability as a tenant; and,

(c) a local connection which exists between a person and the authority's district.[117]

In relation to the third factor at (c) above, readers need to go to section 199 of the Housing Act 1996 to see how "local connection" is defined. Subsection 199(1) provides:

> *"(1) A person has a local connection with the district of a local housing authority if he has a connection with it -*
>
> *(a) because he is, or in the past was, normally resident there, and that residence is or was of his own choice,*[118]
>
> *(b) because he is employed there,*

---

[117] Subsection 166A(5)(a)-(c), Housing Act 1996.

[118] Residence is not of a person's own choice if they, or someone who might reasonably be expected to reside with them, is resident in a district because they are detained under the authority of an Act of Parliament: subsection 199(3), Housing Act 1996.

(c) because of family associations, or

(d) because of special circumstances".[119]

Someone will also have a local connection with the district of a local housing authority if they were, at any time, provided accommodated under section 95 of the Immigration and Asylum Act 1999 in that district.[120] This does not apply, so there will be no local connection, if the person was provided with accommodation in one district and then subsequently provided with section 95, Immigration and Asylum Act 1999 accommodation in another local housing authorities district.[121] It also does not apply where accommodation has been provided in an accommodation centre pursuant to section 22 of the Nationality, Immigration and Asylum Act 2002.[122]

Section 199 of the Housing Act 1996 also makes special provision in relation to some types of children and where their local connection might be. It provides:

> "(8) While a local authority in England[123] have a duty towards a person under section 23C of the Children Act 1989 (continuing functions in respect of former relevant children) -

---

[119] Powers are given to the Secretary of State to specify by order circumstances where a person is not to be treated as employed in a district, or residence in a district is not to be treated as of a person's own choice: subsection 199(5), Housing Act 1996.

[120] Subsection 199(6) of the Housing Act 1996.

[121] Subsection 199(7)(a) of the Housing Act 1996.

[122] Subsection 199(7)(b) of the Housing Act 1996.

[123] In relation to England, "local authority" means "the council of a county, a metropolitan district, a London Borough or the Common Council of the City of London": see section 105 of the Children Act 1989 which is applied to subsection 199(8), Housing Act 1996 by subsection 199(9).

> (a) if the local authority is a local housing authority, the person has a local connection with their district, and
>
> (b) otherwise, the person has a local connection with every district of a local housing authority that falls within the area of the local authority".

Further, if children are in care and provided with accommodation under section 22A of the Children Act 1989 then a person has a local connection with a district if they are normally resident in that district of a local housing authority in England for a continuous period of at least two years and some or all of that person is before the person reaches 16 years of age.[124] A person who has been accommodated under section 22A of the Children Act 1989 will no longer have a local connection, however, where they reach the age of 21.[125] This only applies to the provisions relating to section 22A of the Children Act 1989 contained with section 199 of the Housing Act 1996 and does not therefore prevent such a person, having attained the age of 21, having a local connection under any of the other provisions in section 199, Housing Act 1996.

A scheme may also set out how particular housing accommodation is allocated to a person who makes an application for that specific accommodation or to persons of a particular description,[126] for example, sheltered accommodation or accommodation for specific age groups. This provision allows local housing authorities to operate what have become known as "local lettings policies" so long as the authority can show it has complied with section 166A(3).[127]

---

124 Subsection 199(10), Housing Act 1996.

125 Subsection 199(11), Housing Act 1996.

126 Subsection 166A(6), Housing Act 1996.

127 Allocation of accommodation: guidance for local authorities (https://www.gov.uk/guidance/allocation-of-accommodation-guidance-

It is not unlawful or irrational for local authorities not to give an applicant who falls within more than one of the classes set out in section 166A(3) a choice as to what priority group they should be placed in. This is so even if it means an applicant has less priority that they would do if they were not homeless and in temporary accommodation.[128]

Challenges concerning preference and priorities

There have been a number of cases challenging decisions and policies under section 166A (and its predecessor provisions). As Mr Justice Holman set out in *R (Woolfe) v Islington LBC* [2016] EWHC 1907 (Admin); [2016] HLR 42 at [1]:

> *"The schemes of local housing authorities for allocating their scarce social housing stock seem to be fertile ground for litigation".*

Some cases have been mentioned above. This section sets out some further case examples to help readers see the approach the courts have taken (as well as exploring some of the different ways local authorities decide to give priority to applicants).[129]

One way an allocation scheme can operate is by awarding points to a household in order to given them preference and/or reflect their housing need. This was the type of allocation scheme challenged in *Woolfe*. The London Borough of Islington operated a scheme which set thresholds for the points above which applicants would be eligible to bid. At the time

---

for-local-authorities/chapter-4-framing-an-allocation-scheme) at paragraph 4.21.

128 *R (on the application of Jaberi) v Westminster City Council* [2023] EWHC 1045 (Admin); [2023] PTSR 1402 at [76] to [78]. Please note there is an appeal to the Court of Appeal outstanding.

129 This is not an exhaustive review of the caselaw and focuses on schemes that were challenged rather than the challenge of individual decisions under an allocation scheme.

of the challenge, the points threshold was set at 120.[130] The claimant, who was owed a main housing duty under section 193(2) of Part 7 of the Housing Act 1996, had been awarded 110 points which mean she could not bid for any property even though she was on the housing register.[131] The claimant was given 10 points on account of the homelessness duty owed to her under section 193(2).[132]

Islington also operated a "New Generation scheme" (referenced in the allocation scheme) where additional points could be awarded if an applicant was living as an agreed member of the household of an Islington resident for a continuous block of at least three years within the last five years.[133] Prior to her homelessness approach and application to join Islington's housing register, the claimant was living with her mother in a flat in Islington's area. At the time the authority made a decision on her application to join the housing register under Part 6 of the Housing Act 1996, the claimant was no longer living with her mother and Islington did not consider whether or not she should have been awarded points under its New Generation scheme.[134]

The challenge to the points based allocation scheme was that using a threshold was unlawful either under section 166A and/or because it had been *"adopted and maintained"* in breach of section 11 of the Children Act 2004.[135] The claimant also averred that Islington should have

---

130 *R (Woolfe) v Islington LBC* [2016] EWHC 1907 (Admin); [2016] HLR 42 at [9].

131 *Ibid* at [10].

132 *Ibid* at [5].

133 *Ibid* at [70].

134 *Ibid* at [3]-[5] and [56].

135 *Ibid* at [13] and [51]. Section 11(2) of the Children Act 2004 provides: *"(2) Each … body [which includes a local authority] to whom this section applies must make arrangements for ensuring that – (a) their functions are*

considered the claimant for a points award under the New Generation scheme and had erred in its decision not to do so.

In relation to the arguments by the claimants under section 166A under the Housing Act 1996 and section 11 of the Children Act 2004, the Court held that the scheme was lawful. Islington was wrong, however, not to have considered the claimant for points under the New Generation scheme. The claim was allowed.

First, the points threshold did not offend section 166A. Islington had an allocation scheme which set out the procedure that would be followed and gave reasonable preference to the specified classes of person. In terms of those applicants who were homeless and should be given preference, 10 points were awarded.[136] The court, applying *R (Lin) v Barnet LBC* [2007] EWCA Civ 132; [2007] HLR 30[137] and *R (Ahmad) v Newham London BC* [2009] UKHL 14; [2009] 3 All E.R. 755,[138] held:

> *"38. ...the policy and decision of the housing authority to award 10 points for homelessness does fulfil their statutory duty to secure that preference is given to the claimant, and I cannot adjudicate on the reasonableness of the preference so given. In my view, the setting of the bidding threshold is a different aspect of the overall allocation process, not itself concerned with the issue of preference or priorities. Preference has already been assessed by the awarding of points.*

---

discharged having regard to the need to safeguard and promote the welfare of children; ...".

136 *R (Woolfe) v Islington LBC* [2016] EWHC 1907 (Admin); [2016] HLR 42 at [36]-[37].

137 The Court specifically referred to Dyson LJ in *Lin* at 451, [27]-[28] where he said: "... *a person who has 10 points is in a better position to bid than a person who does not have 10 points. He is accorded preference ... whether the preference is 'reasonable' ... is a matter for the discretion of the council*".

138 Referencing [16], [46] and [62] of *Ahmad.*

> *39. …*
>
> *40. It was in my view entirely lawful for Islington to decide…that a threshold assists in managing the bidding process by limiting the volume of applicants who are bidding to those who have a realistic chance of actually being rehoused under the scheme. They keep the level of their threshold under review by monitoring it. The level at which they set their threshold is a matter for their judgment, not that of the court".*

Secondly, the Court held Islington's welfare category within its allocation scheme and the fact that it is considered in individual cases was broad enough so as to have regard to the need to safeguard and promote the welfare of children as required by section 11 of the Children Act 2004. The allocation of points was not inconsistent with the duty under section 11.[139]

Finally, Islington had misapplied its New Generation scheme and, as such, the decision was quashed so as to allow the authority to consider whether or not the claimant met the criteria for that scheme.[140]

Both parties applied for permission to appeal to the Court of Appeal. This was refused.[141]

It should also be noted, however, that Islington's scheme of 120 threshold points, was challenged again in *R (C) v Islington LBC* [2017] EWHC 1288 (Admin); [2017] HLR 32. In so far as the scheme did not

---

139 *R (Woolfe) v Islington LBC* [2016] EWHC 1907 (Admin); [2016] HLR 42 at [52].

140 *Ibid* at [63], [68]-69.

141 *Woolfe v London Brough of Islington* [2017] EWCA Civ 2027.

set out the criteria used to make direct offers, the procedure within the allocations scheme for making direct offers was unlawful.[142]

In terms of priorities, some housing allocation schemes use length of residence with the authority's area as a way to prioritise people on its housing register. Such an approach was challenged in the conjoined appeals of *R (on the application of Gullu) v Hillingdon LBC* and *R (on the application of Ward) v Hillingdon LBC* [2019] EWCA Civ 692; [2019] PTSR 1738.[143] In those cases, the London Borough of Hillingdon operated an allocation scheme which did not allow a person to join the housing register if that person had not been continuously living in the borough for at least 10 years ("the residence requirement"). Where a person was unintentionally homeless but did not meet the residence requirement, they would be entitled to join the register but would be placed into band D.[144]

In the two cases, the lawfulness of the residence requirement was challenged by Irish Travellers[145] and a Kurdish refugee of Turkish nationality.[146] The challenges focused on whether or not the scheme – which was the provision, criterion or practice ("PCP") challenged – indirectly discriminated under sections 19 and 29 of the Equality Act

142 *R (C) v Islington LBC* [2017] EWHC 1288 (Admin); [2017] HLR 32 at [61]-[63].

143 See also *R (on the application of H) v Ealing LBC* [2017] EWCA Civ 1127; [2018] PTSR 541 which was followed in *Gullu* and *Ward.*

144 *R (on the application of Gullu) v Hillingdon LBC* and *R (on the application of Ward) v Hillingdon LBC* [2019] EWCA Civ 692; [2019] PTSR 1738 at [1].

145 The Irish Travellers succeeded at first instance: *R (TW) v London Borough of Hillingdon* [2018] EWHC 1791 (Admin); [2018] PTSR 1678.

146 This challenged was unsuccessful at first instance: *R (Gullu) v London Borough of Hillingdon* [2018] EWHC 1937 (Admin); [2019] HLR 4.

2010.[147] Section 19 of the Equality Act 2010, so far as is relevant, provides:

> "(1) A person (A) discriminates against another (B) if A applies to B a provision, criterion or practice which is discriminatory in relation to a relevant protected characteristic of B's.
>
> (2) For the purposes of subsection (1), a provision, criterion or practice is discriminatory in relation to a relevant protected characteristic of B's if –
>
> > (a) A applies, or would apply, it to persons with whom B does not share the characteristic,
> >
> > (b) it puts, or would put, persons with whom B shares the characteristic at a particular disadvantage when compared with persons with whom B does not share it,
> >
> > (c) it puts, or would put, B at that disadvantage, and

---

[147] There were also arguments:

a. that Hillingdon were in breach of the public-sector equality duty (PSED) under section 149 of the Equality Act 2010. The court held Hillingdon was not in breach of that duty initially but Mr Gullu has established a breach of the PSED as, once he has raised it, Hillingdon ought to have considered the position of non-UK nationals;

b. in the case of *Ward,* that Hillingdon were in breach of the Children Act 2004. The Court held there has been no such breach; and,

c. that Mr Gullu had a particular status under article 14 of the European Convention on Human Rights and that article 8 was engaged. This question was left for another day: see *R (on the application of Gullu) v Hillingdon LBC* and *R (on the application of Ward) v Hillingdon LBC* [2019] EWCA Civ 692; [2019] PTSR 1738 at [74] and [102]-[109].

(d) A cannot show it to be a proportionate means of achieving a legitimate aim".

The protected characteristic relied upon was race which is a relevant protected characteristic under section 19 of the Equality Act 2010.[148] Hillingdon had carried out two equality impact assessments before formulating the scheme.[149]

Ultimately, after the Court held that the PCP (the allocation scheme) did indirectly discriminate against Irish Travellers and non-UK nationals,[150] the matter came down to whether or not Hillingdon could justify the indirect discrimination. There were two issues:

- whether the policy, taken as a whole, contained sufficient safeguards to eliminate the indirect discrimination resulting from the impugned PCP; and,

- whether any indirect discrimination was justified.[151]

The burden to answer the above questions was on Hillingdon as the maker of the policy.[152] It did not discharge that burden, the scheme as a

---

148 Under subsections 9(1) and (4) of the Equality Act 2010 "Race" includes colour, nationality and ethnic or national origins but a racial group may consist of two or more distinct racial groups.

149 *R (on the application of Gullu) v Hillingdon LBC* and *R (on the application of Ward) v Hillingdon LBC* [2019] EWCA Civ 692; [2019] PTSR 1738 at [22]-[32].

150 *Ibid* at [89].

151 *Ibid* at [75].

152 *Ibid* at [76].

whole did not eliminate the discrimination and the indirect discrimination had *"not yet been justified"*.[153]

A similar challenge was seen in *R (H) v Ealing LBC* [2017] EWCA Civ 1127; [2018] PTSR 541 which was cited and followed in *Gullu* and *Ward.* The Ealing case concerned those who could work.[154] In that case, Ealing introduced an allocations scheme in October 2013 which provided for two priority schemes:

> "2. Applicants who work or adhere to the rules in conducting their Council tenancy;
>
>> 20% of lettings will be made available to applicants from working households and those Council tenants who comply with their tenancy agreement and pay their rent and council tax.
>>
>> Working households will only qualify if they have been employed for a minimum of 24 hours a week and for 12 out of the last 18 months. Evidence of employment will be required in the form of tax returns, copy of employment contract and/or any other suitable proof as requested.
>>
>> Ealing Council has a scheme which rewards good tenants who want the opportunity to seek a transfer. These transfer applicants are existing tenants who have demonstrated that

---

153 *Ibid* at [87]-[88], [96]-[97] and [113]-[114].

154 See also *R (XC) v Southwark LBC* [2017] EWHC 736 (Admin); [2017] HLR 24 which concerned the rights of disabled persons and women where Southwark's allocation scheme awarded a priority star when an applicant was in work. Whilst this did indirectly discriminate under section 19 of the Equality Act 2010 against disabled persons and women with child care who were less likely to be in work, it could be justified. The claim was dismissed: at [74]-[77], [85]-[86] and [97]-[100].

> they are 'model' tenants by complying with their tenancy agreement for a specified period of time.
>
> In order to bid successfully for properties advertised as part of this scheme, Households:
>
> (a) Must not have rent arrears for the previous 12 months.
>
> (b) Must not have breached their tenancy conditions for the previous two years.
>
> (c) Must not have any anti-social behaviour record.
>
> Once tenants have been accepted for the scheme they must continue to comply with the above criteria until they are rehoused in order to remain with the scheme.
>
> Applications will be prioritised by band and date within that band … ."[155]

The above is referred to as the "Working Household Priority Scheme" and, whilst finding that it gave rise to indirect discrimination against disabled persons and older people who were less likely to work under section 19 of the Equality Act 2010, the Court held the scheme could be justified *i.e.* when the scheme as a whole was considered, it was a proportionate means of achieving a legitimate aim.[156]

---

155 *R (H) v Ealing LBC* [2017] EWCA Civ 1127; [2018] PTSR 541 at [8].

156 *Ibid* at [57]-[59], [82], [127] and [131].

Allocation schemes have also been challenged using articles 14 and 8 of the European Convention on Human Rights but there is still some uncertainty as to what Convention rights are engaged when it comes to issues of allocation.[157]

[157] There are some Administrative Court cases where the engagement of article 8, ECHR has been accepted (see *e.g. R(HA) v Ealing LBC* [2015] EWHC 2375 (Admin); [2016] PTSR 16 and *R (on the application of Fartun Osman) v London Borough of Harrow* [2017] EWHC 274 (Admin) (where the parties agreed it was engaged)). In *R (H) v Ealing LBC* [2017] EWCA Civ 1127; [2018] PTSR 541, however, this was doubted. It was also doubted by the Court of Appeal in *R (on the application of Z) v Hackney LBC* [2019] EWCA Civ 1099; [2019] PTSR 2272 but, the Supreme Court in *R (on the application of Z) v Hackney LBC* [2020] UKSC 40; [2020] 1 WLR 4327 at [52], [96]-[97], [116] expressed its doubts of the Court of Appeal's conclusion on this point.

CHAPTER FIVE

ALLOCATION SCHEMES

As discussed earlier in this book, under section 166A of the Housing Act 1996 every local housing authority in England must have a scheme dealing with the allocation of housing accommodation. This applies even if a local housing authority does not have its own housing stock. It also applies if a local authority has contracted out certain functions under Part 6 (which is discussed below). Subject to the provisions set out in subsections 166A(1) to (10) of the Housing Act 1996 (and any regulations made under subsection 166A(10)), a local housing authority may decide on what principles its allocation scheme is to be framed.[158]

Housing accommodation must then be allocated in accordance with the scheme.[159] The scheme must not only contain information as to how the local housing authority determines priorities for the allocation of housing; it must also contain the procedure to be followed.

This chapter specifically looks at the formalities of the scheme itself and readers are reminded that all the chapters in this book are relevant to what an allocation scheme must contain and how it should be framed. Readers will also find Chapters 4 and 5 of the statutory guidance for local authorities helpful on framing and managing an allocation scheme.

The procedure

As touched upon above, section 166A(1) provides that an allocation scheme not only needs to set out how priorities are determined but also needs to contain the procedure to be followed by the local housing

158 Section 166A(11), Housing Act 1996.

159 Section 166A(14), Housing Act 1996.

authority. The section defines "procedure" and states that it *"includes all aspects of the allocation process, including the persons or descriptions of persons by whom decisions are taken"*. It is not, therefore, necessarily an easy document to put together. The scheme will need to contain an awful lot of detail in a user friendly manner. Not only should it be clear to those within a local authority applying the scheme what should be done, when and by whom but it also needs to be clear to applicants. If local housing authorities use job descriptions or job titles in relation to those that are taking decisions, it needs to be careful to ensure such information remains relevant and updated should there be name changes to such roles and descriptions.

In relation to the procedure to be followed, the scheme must be framed in accordance with any principles prescribed by the Secretary of State set out in regulations.[160]

Statement of policy

An allocation scheme needs to include a statement of the local housing authority's policy on offering people who are to be allocated housing accommodation a choice of such accommodation or the opportunity to express preferences about the housing accommodation to be allocated to them: section 166A(2), Housing Act 1996. It is for the local authority to set its policy on these matters.

Reasonable and additional preference

Subject to certain provisions regarding restricted persons, any allocation scheme must be framed so as to give reasonable preference to certain categories of applicants.[161] There is also a power for a local housing authority to give additional preference to categories of people.[162] Section

---

160 Subsection 166A(10), Housing Act 1996.

161 Subsections 166A(3)(a)-(e) and (4), Housing Act 1996.

162 Subsections 166A(3)(i)-(iv), Housing Act 1996.

166A(3), however, dictates that an allocation scheme must give additional preference to certain categories of people linked to the armed forces. Reasonable and additional preference has its own dedicated chapter in this book and readers should look at Chapter 4 for more detail. The content of that chapter is not repeated here.

Determining priorities

Where a person is given a reasonable or additional preference, an allocation scheme may set out how priorities are determined in relation to allocating housing to such persons[163] *i.e.* a local authority can specify how households with a similar level of need (or preference) are 'ranked' when it is considering who should get an allocation of housing. One common way of determining priorities is by reference to the date upon which an applicant joined the housing register.

Section 166A(5) sets out examples of the type of things a local housing authority may wish to take into account when making such decisions. The factors suggested in section 166A(5) are: (a) the financial resources available to an applicant to meet housing costs; (b) any behaviour of an applicant (or of a member of their household) which could affect their suitability to be a tenant; and, (c) any local connection which exists between the applicant and the local authority's district. It is important to recognised that what the examples within section 166A(5) *"do not do is to altogether remove [those categories of person to which reasonable preference must be given] from the potential of being allocated social housing"*.[164] Section 166A(5) essentially allows the local authority to create a sub-group, from a larger group that must be given reasonable preference, in

[163] Subsection 166A(5), Housing Act 1996.

[164] *R (on the application of Alemi) v Westminster City Council* [2015] EWHC 1765 (Admin); [2015] PTSR 1339 at [29].

relation to which the authority may justify a difference in the priority they are given within that larger group.[165]

The statutory guidance for local authorities also encourages local housing authorities to include local priorities alongside the statutory reasonable preference categories. This is another example of the flexibility and discretion given to local housing authorities to set the parameters of their scheme to the benefit of the needs of their areas. An authority needs to be careful so as to ensure that non-statutory priorities, or preferences, do not dominate an allocation scheme.[166] This is discussed in more detailed in Chapter 4.

Information

Section 166A(9) of the Housing Act 1996 demands that any allocation scheme is framed so as to ensure that an applicant has the right to request certain information about the scheme, decisions and reviews.[167]

This includes a scheme being framed so as to include a right to request general information to enable the applicant to assess:

(a) how their application is likely to be treated under the local housing authority's scheme; and

(b) whether housing accommodation appropriate to their needs is likely to be made available and, if so, how long it is likely to take before such accommodation becomes available for allocation to the applicant. In relation to this aspect, the statutory guidance for

165 *R (on the application of Alemi) v Westminster City Council* [2015] EWHC 1765 (Admin); [2015] PTSR 1339 at [29].

166 See paragraph 4.19 of the statutory guidance for local authorities which cites *R (on the Application of Ahmad) v Newham LBC* [2009] UKHL 14; [2009] PTSR 632.

167 Section 166A(9).

local authorities at paragraph 5.6, encourages the use and maintenance of a database of suitable housing for those with access needs. It is said this would assist to provide the information required under this part of section 166 when read with section 166A(9) of the Housing Act 1996. Most local housing authorities maintain housing databases and this suggestion could be extrapolated so as to enable authorities to filter accommodation so as to provide information about suitable accommodation for those with particular needs (not just limited to access).

The other rights set out in section 166A(9) of the Housing Act 1996 which a local housing authority must inform an applicant about are:

(a) the right to request that the authority inform the applicant of any decision about the facts of his case that have been or are likely to be taken into account in considering whether to allocate housing accommodation to them; and

(b) the right to request a review of a decision taken under paragraph (b), or in section 160ZA(9) of the Housing Act 1996, and to be informed of the decision on the review and the grounds for it.[168]

Preparing, and making changes to, an allocation scheme

Subsection 166A(12) of the Housing Act 1996 sets out what a local housing authority must have regard to when it is either preparing or modifying its allocation scheme Those matters include the following two strategies which local authorities should have in place:

(a) a current homelessness strategy pursuant to section 1 of the Homelessness Act 2002; and,

[168] Section 166(1A) and section 166A(9) of the Housing Act 1996. See also Chapter 6 for a discussion as to the review process which should be set out in any allocation scheme.

(b) a current tenancy strategy in place pursuant to section 150 of the Localism Act 2011.

London borough councils must also have regard to the London housing strategy.

Before adopting an allocation scheme, a local housing authority must send a copy of the draft scheme to every PRPSH and RSL with which they have nomination arrangements (see below) and any other person who should be afforded with a reasonable opportunity to comment on the scheme.[169] A local housing authority will, therefore, need to think carefully about bringing an allocation scheme to the attention of those it will affect in the community.

These provisions also apply where an allocation scheme already in place is going to be modified so as to reflect a "major change" of policy. In those circumstances, the local housing authority need only send the proposed changes to any relevant PRPSH, RSL and persons who should be afforded with a reasonable opportunity to comment on the proposal.[170] By way of example, the statutory guidance for local authorities suggests, at paragraph 5.2, that a *"major policy change would include…any amendment affecting the relative priority of a large number of applicants or a significant alteration to procedures"*. In contrast, where a scheme made provision for preference to be kept under review it was held that a need to vary targets in the light of preference or to meet a change of circumstances was not a major policy change.[171]

There is actually no statutory obligation to keep the terms of an allocation scheme under review or to revise it regularly but this is encouraged, to a

---

[169] Subsection 166A(13), Housing Act 1996.

[170] Subsection 166A(13), Housing Act 1996.

[171] *R (A) v Lambeth LBC* [2002] EWCA Civ 1084, [2002] HLR 57 at [26]-[28]. It should be noted that Lambeth's allocation scheme was held to be unlawful.

certain extent, by the statutory guidance for local authorities. Local authorities should, however, keep a close eye on changes to the following.

- Legislation (including regulations). This not only means keeping an eye on any changes to Part 6 of the Housing Act 1985 but includes other amendments to any other statutory regimes which will feed into allocations schemes, for example, local authorities duties in relation to those with protected characteristics under the Equality Act 2010 and other vulnerable groups (as discussed below).

- Statutory guidance. It can be seen throughout this book that there is not only general statutory guidance as to the allocation of social housing but there is specific guidance dealing with particular groups of people.

- Decisions of the courts.

Keeping an eye on the above will allow local housing authorities to assess whether or not changes need to be made to their allocation schemes.

There are a number of other public law duties, some of which are outside the scope of this book, which should be considered when a local housing authority is developing or changing an allocations scheme. Such duties include the following.

(a) Carrying out an impact assessment and, in particular, considering the Equality Act 2010 and any policies on equality that the local authority has in place.

(b) Section 11 of the Children Act 2004 which sets out a duty on local authorities when discharging their functions to make arrangements to ensure they have regard *"to the need to safeguard and promote the welfare of children"*.[172]

(c) Section 343AA of the Armed Forces Act 2006 which places a duty on local authorities carrying out a housing function of having "due regard" to the:

- unique obligations of, and sacrifices made by, the armed forces;
- the desirability of removing disadvantages arising from service in the armed forces; and,
- the principle that special provision may be justified.

Where an allocation scheme is amended and applicants have already applied and been assessed under the old scheme, the new or modified scheme needs to make it clear how such applicants are to be treated under the new/amended scheme.[173]

---

[172] Whilst not a decision under Part 6 of the Housing Act 1996, see generally, *Nzolameso v Westminster City Council* [2015] UKSC 22, [2015] 2 All ER 942 at [22]-[30] and [38]-[39] for a helpful discussion on section 11 if the Children Act 2004. The obligation under section 11 may be satisfied by discussions with the social services department of a local authority before implementing a new or modified allocation scheme: see *R (Woolfe) v Islington LBC* [2016] EWHC 1907 (Admin); [2016] HLR 42. In that case, *Islington* had a joint working protocol in place between its Children's services and housing department and it had complied with its duties under section 11 of the Children Act 2004 when setting the points threshold within its allocation scheme.

[173] See, by way of example, *R (Faarah) v Southwark LBC* [2008] EWCA Civ 807; [2009] HLR 12, CA.

Publication of the scheme

A summary of the allocation scheme must be published by a local housing authority. Local authorities should also:

(a) provide a copy of the summary of the scheme free of charge to any member of the public who asks for one;

(b) make the scheme available for inspection at their principal office; and,

(c) provide a copy of the scheme to any member of the public who asks for one for which a reasonable fee can be charged with the copy being provided on payment of the fee.[174]

When there is a major change of policy, there is also a requirement for a local housing authority to take any steps it considers reasonable to bring the effect of such amendment to the attention of those likely to be affected by it within a reasonable period of time.[175]

Guidance by the Secretary of State.

As set out in previous chapters, local housing authorities are required by section 169, Housing Act 1996 to have regard to any guidance as may from time to time be given by the Secretary of State when exercising functions under Part 6, Housing Act 1996.

Whilst already mentioned throughout this book, the current statutory guidance to which local housing authorities should have regard is as follows.

---

[174] Subsections 168 (1) and (2), Housing Act 1996.

[175] Subsection 168(3), Housing Act 1996.

- Allocation of accommodation: guidance for local authorities, 27 October 2023;

- Providing social housing for local people, 31 December 2013;

- Right to Move and social housing allocations, 27 March 2015;

- Improving access to social housing for victims of domestic abuse, 25 January 2022; and,

- Improving access to social housing for members of the Armed Forces, 27 June 2020.[176]

Co-operation, nomination and contracting out

Under section 170, Housing Act 1996, there needs to be cooperation between certain social landlords and local housing authorities. The section provides that *"where a local housing authority so request, a private registered provider of social housing or registered social landlord shall co-operate to such extent as is reasonable in the circumstances in offering accommodation to people with priority under the authority's allocation scheme"*.

Local housing authorities are likely to have nomination agreements in place with private registered providers so as to assist in meeting the obligations under Part 6, Housing Act 1996.[177]

---

[176] The statutory guidance can be found here: https://www.gov.uk/government/collections/social-housing-allocations-guidance.

[177] See subsection 159(4), Housing Act 1996 and paragraphs 6.2 to 6.4 of the statutory guidance for local authorities.

Local authorities can also contract out certain functions which includes some functions in relation to the allocation of social housing. Under paragraph 2 of the Local Authorities (Contracting Out of Allocation of Housing and Homelessness Functions) Order 1996:[178]

> *"Any function of an authority which is conferred by or under Part [6] of the Act (allocation of housing accommodation), except one which is listed in Schedule 1 to this Order, may be exercised by, or by employees of, such person (if any) as may be authorised in that behalf by the authority whose function it is".*

The result of schedule 1 of the 1996 Order is that the following cannot be contracted out.

- Adopting or altering an allocation scheme (including decisions as to the principles on which the scheme is framed) and consulting private registered providers.

- Making the allocation scheme available for inspection at the authority's principal office.[179]

Challenge

There are a number of examples throughout this book of successful and unsuccessful challenges to allocation schemes. As a general principle, where a housing allocation scheme complies with the statutory requirements of section 166A(3) and any other statutory requirements, the courts should be very slow to interfere on the ground of alleged irrationality.[180]

---

[178] SI No. 3205.

[179] See also paragraph 6.6. of the statutory guidance for local authorities.

[180] *R (on the Application of Ahmad) v Newham LBC* [2009] UKHL 14; [2009] PTSR 632 at [55] *per* Lord Neuberger.

CHAPTER SIX

APPLICATIONS FOR HOUSING ACCOMMODATION

Advice, information and an applicant's rights

Under section 166 of the Housing Act 1996, a local housing authority is to make sure that advice and information about the right to make an application for an allocation of housing accommodation is available to people in their district. Such information and advice is to be made available free of charge. The statutory guidance for local authorities[181] sets out, at paragraph 5.4, that this obligations includes information about the procedures to apply for an allocation and qualification and prioritisation criteria.

Moreover, where anyone in a local authority's district may have a difficulty in accessing such information or advice without assistance, the local housing authority shall ensure that any necessary assistance is available, again free of charge, to such persons.

A local housing authority in England must also inform an applicant for an allocation of the rights set out in section 166A(9) of the Housing Act 1996. This has been discussed in Chapter 5.

---

[181] *Allocation of accommodation: guidance for local authorities*, Department for Levelling Up, Housing and Communities, published 29 June 2012 and updated 15 May 2023.

Considering an application for an allocation of housing

It is perhaps obvious to say but, if there was any doubt, section 166(3) of the Housing Act 1996 makes it plain that a local housing authority must consider every application made to it (provided the application is made in accordance with any procedural requirements under the authority's allocation scheme).

On 1 April 1997, the Allocation of Housing (Procedure) Regulations 1997[182] came into force. Regulation 3(2) makes it clear that an elected member is not to be involved in any decision-making as to the allocation of social housing.[183] This applies in relation to a:

"member of an authority who has been elected for the electoral division or ward in which –

> *(a) the housing accommodation in relation to which an allocation decision falls to be made is situated, or*
>
> *(b) the person in relation to whom that decision falls to be made has his sole or main residence".*

As set out in the statutory guidance for local authorities[184] at paragraph 5.13, the Allocation of Housing (Procedure) Regulations 1997 do not prevent such an elected member from:

- representing their constituents in front of the local authority's decision-making body; or,

---

182 SI No. 483.

183 Regulation 3(2), Allocation of Housing (Procedure) Regulations 1997.

184 *Allocation of accommodation: guidance for local authorities*, Department for Levelling Up, Housing and Communities, published 29 June 2012 and updated 15 May 2023.

- taking part in the deliberations prior to the decision-making body's decision; or,

- being involved in matters of policy that impact upon the *"generality of housing accommodation"* within their area *i.e.* the regulations are aimed at individual decisions and cases rather than broader issues of policy.

Disclosure, personal data and safeguarding when dealing with applications

The fact a person is an applicant for an allocation of housing accommodation shall not (without that person's consent) be disclosed to any other member of the public. The wording used in section 166(4) is that such information should not be "divulged". Although "disclosure" is used in this part, it is not being used as a term of art.

As set out in the statutory guidance for local authorities[185] at paragraphs 5.8 to 5.11, it is important for local housing authority's to be alert to any safeguarding concerns and how this relates to any information provided, gathered and/or processed in the course of an application for an allocation of housing. Within the statutory guidance, there is a sobering case study as to what happens when safeguarding, or the lack of it, goes wrong. Local housing authorities are reminded that there is also statutory guidance – which compliments the allocation statutory guidance – available as to how to support victims of domestic abuse.[186] The Improving access to social housing for victims of domestic abuse statutory guidance stresses, amongst other things, the importance of

[185] *Allocation of accommodation: guidance for local authorities*, Department for Levelling Up, Housing and Communities, published 29 June 2012 and updated 15 May 2023.

[186] Improving access to social housing for victims of domestic abuse, Secretary of State for Housing, Communities and Local Government, updated 25 January 2022.

working with other agencies and using best practice to keep victims of abuse safe.

Local housing authorities should also remember their duties under any relevant data protection laws so as to ensure personal data is processed and held in accordance with the law. Authorities are reminded of these duties at paragraph 5.7 of the statutory guidance for local authorities[187] and when some information can be shared on a lawful basis.[188]

Paragraph 5.8 of the statutory guidance directs local housing authorities to the Information Commissioner[189] or their own data protection teams should there be any doubt as to what they can and cannot in the individual circumstances. In particular the statutory guidance considers safeguarding concerns and sets out, again at paragraph 5.8, that:

"Local Housing Authorities should consider whether it is appropriate to share information regarding safeguarding concerns, including, but not limited to concerns about domestic violence and abuse, with other agencies (such as housing associations and GP surgeries). It is the responsibility of Local Housing Authorities to determine whether data sharing is lawful under UK data protection law. Whether data sharing is lawful must be determined on a case-by-case basis".

Giving false information during the course of an application for housing

If an applicant gives false information on an application for an allocation of housing, this can have extremely serious consequences; it is a criminal offence. Allocation schemes should make the rules and the consequences

---

187 *Allocation of accommodation: guidance for local authorities*, Department for Levelling Up, Housing and Communities, published 29 June 2012 and updated 15 May 2023.

188 The ins and outs of data protection law is outside the scope of this book.

189 See generally www.ico.org.uk for guidance.

of breach of those rules clear to the applicant. A local housing authority may also wish to include a declaration as to the truthfulness of an application on any form that is part of its application processes and procedures.

The rules, making clear a person commits an offence, come from section 171 of the Housing Act 1996 which provides:

> *"(1) A person commits an offence if, in connection with the exercise by a local housing authority of their functions under [Part 6] -*
>
> > *(a) he knowingly or recklessly makes a statement which is false in a material particular, or*
> >
> > *(b) he knowingly withholds information which the authority have reasonably required him to give in connection with the exercise of those functions.*
>
> *(2) A person guilty of an offence under this section is liable on summary conviction to a fine not exceeding level 5 on the standard scale".*

The offence covers material reckless statements which are false as well as knowingly withholding information which an authority has reasonably sought from an applicant. The offence is summary which means any case would be dealt with by the Magistrates' Court. For offences committed after 13 March 2015, the statutory limit for a level 5 fine is unlimited. For offences committed prior to 15 March 2015, the level 5 maximum is £5,000.

If an allocation is made and it is later discovered that the terms of section 171 of the Housing Act 1996 are met, there are grounds for possession which mirrors the language of section 171. Ground 5, schedule 2 of the Housing Act 1985 (secure tenancies) and ground 17, schedule 2 of the Housing Act 1988 (assured tenancies) provide a ground for possession where:

"The tenant is the person, or one of the persons, to whom the tenancy was granted and the landlord was induced to grant the tenancy by a false statement made knowingly or recklessly by –

(a) the tenant, or

(b) a person acting at the tenant's instigation".

The grounds for possession, as with section 171 of the Housing Act 1996, not only extend to false representations known to be false at the time of making, but also to "reckless" statements. Even if ground 5 or ground 17 is made out, a court would still have to find it reasonable to make a possession order *i.e.* there is a discretion as to whether or not a possession order is made.[190]

The case of *Waltham Forest LBC v Roberts* [2005] H.L.R. 2 demonstrates how a false statement made before a tenancy is granted, for example on an application for an allocation of housing, can impact on ground 5, schedule 2, Housing Act 1985 (which will also be relevant to ground 17, schedule 2, Housing Act 1988). In *Roberts*, it was held that if any statement made before a tenancy was granted is material, the court should infer that that statement did induce the landlord to grant the relevant tenancy. One common issue where the allocation of housing is concerned is an applicant not declaring ownership of another property. In *Roberts,* Newman J said at [42] and [43]:

(a) that *"in connection with a housing application the applicant's ownership of a property is obviously material"*; and.

(b) *"[o]nce materiality has been established it is a 'fair inference' of fact that the misrepresentee has been influenced by the statement".*

[190] Possession proceedings (including the grounds for possession) are outside the scope of this book.

The statutory guidance for local authorities[191] at paragraph 5.15 notes an offence could be committed where false information is given on an application form for social housing, in response to a request for further information in support of the application and/or during any review proceedings.

Unfortunately, the allocation of social housing based upon false or incorrect information to those who are not eligible and/or do not qualify is not limited to problems with an applicant themselves giving such information. There can also be issues caused by those employed by a local housing authority.

The statutory guidance for local authorities[192] at paragraph 5.17 highlights the potential problem with applications that may be tainted by the conduct of an employee of the local housing authority. The statutory guidance for local authorities advises that authorities *"may …wish to take action to minimise the risk of staff allocating incorrectly or even fraudulently, for example to applicants who do not have sufficient priority under the allocation scheme or do not meet the authority's qualification criteria. Appropriate steps might include vetting staff who take allocation decisions or providing for decisions to be validated by employing senior staff to undertake random checks"*.

Birmingham City Council v Qasim [2009] EWCA Civ 1080; [2010] PTSR 471 is a case which provides a stark example of employee wrongdoing in the allocation of social housing. In *Qasim*, Birmingham City Council had cause to investigate following a discovery that an officer employed in their housing department had been granting secure

---

[191] *Allocation of accommodation: guidance for local authorities*, Department for Levelling Up, Housing and Communities, published 29 June 2012 and updated 15 May 2023.

[192] *Allocation of accommodation: guidance for local authorities*, Department for Levelling Up, Housing and Communities, published 29 June 2012 and updated 15 May 2023.

tenancies without applying the criteria set out in its allocation scheme. The tenancies had been granted to persons who did not have priority but Birmingham City Council did not find, and so could not establish, any payment being made (or other improper inducement or benefit being proffered or given) to the officer.[193]

Local housing authorities are under a duty to observe the statutory rules regarding the allocation of residential tenancies. In most cases, they also have limited housing stock (some local authorities do not hold any of their own stock) which is in high demand *i.e.* there is a large number of people, who do qualify for an allocation, waiting on a list for accommodation. In such circumstances, it is prudent for local housing authorities to heed the advice given in paragraph 5.17 of the statutory guidance for local authorities so allocations are made lawfully and they do not find themselves in the same position as Birmingham City Council found itself in in *Qasim*.

Decisions on applications

As set out in Chapter 2, subsections 160ZA(9) and (10) provide that a local housing authority shall notify a person of any decision that the person is ineligible or does not qualify for an allocation of housing accommodation. The notice, which must give "clear grounds" for the decision based on the relevant facts of the applicant case,[194] shall be in writing. If an applicant does not receive the decision, it will be treated as given if the decision was made available for collection (either by the application or by someone on their behalf) at the local authority's offices for a reasonable period of time.

---

[193] *Birmingham City Council v Qasim* [2009] EWCA Civ 1080; [2010] PTSR 471 at [2] to [4].

[194] Paragraph 5.20 of the *Allocation of accommodation: guidance for local authorities*, Department for Levelling Up, Housing and Communities, published 29 June 2012 and updated 15 May 2023.

Although not a statutory requirement, local housing authorities are told at paragraph 5.20 of the statutory guidance for local authorities[195] that it would be good practice to make arrangements for information to be explained to an applicant who may have difficulty in understanding a decision on qualification and/or eligibility. This may be engaged in a large number of cases as it is not straightforward. The suggestion is that an explanation is given verbally. Such decisions can be complicated and so it makes sense to offer such an additional arrangement. If an explanation is given orally, the local housing authority should record that fact. Local housing authorities are reminded, however, that any such step is in addition to providing the notice in writing; it is not an "either/or" option under the legal framework or the statutory guidance for local authorities.

Reviews

In Chapter 5, it was explained that an allocation scheme must contain the procedure to be followed in respect of applications. The procedure includes the local housing authority's review procedure. The procedures should be clear, fair, transparent and include timescales. The statutory guidance for local authorities[196] at paragraph 5.23 sets out general principles which it says reflect good practice. Local housing authorities should have regard to these paragraphs when framing their procedures. The general principles set out in the statutory guidance for local authorities are as follows.

(a) Timescales. 21 days from the date of notification of the decision is a reasonable and well-established timeframe for an applicant to

---

195 *Allocation of accommodation: guidance for local authorities*, Department for Levelling Up, Housing and Communities, published 29 June 2012 and updated 15 May 2023.

196 *Allocation of accommodation: guidance for local authorities*, Department for Levelling Up, Housing and Communities, published 29 June 2012 and updated 15 May 2023.

request a review. In terms of being "well-established", readers may recognise such a timescale from section 202(3) of the Housing Act 1996 (section 202 deals with the right to request a review of certain decision taken under Part 7 of the Housing Act 1996, Homelessness: England). Applicants should be notified of the timescale within which they must request a review. A local housing authority can and should retain a discretion to extend any time limit they set where there are exceptional circumstances.

(b) Form of request. The guidance provides that applicants should be notified that the request for review should be made in writing. It should also be made clear that it would be acceptable for a request to be made by a representative on an applicant's behalf. If a local housing authority requires specific information to be provided on request for a review, an applicant should be advised of the need for such information and what should be included.

(c) Form of representations. Consideration should be given as to whether or not verbal, as well as written, representations can be made. A local housing authority should advise as to how representations may, or are to, be made.

(d) Who carries out the review.[197] If a local authority decides one person is to make the decision on review, that officer should be senior to the person who made the original decision. Alternatively, local housing authorities may decide to appoint a panel to consider the review. If a panel is appointed, the person who made the original decision should not be on the panel.

(e) What to take into account on review. A review decision should be made in accordance with, and consider, the local housing

---

[197] See Chapter 5 for the definition of "procedure" within section 166A(1) of the Housing Act 1996 and a scheme containing information about those who will make decisions under the scheme.

authority's allocation scheme, any legal framework and all relevant information. In relation to the latter, this will include information since the original decision was made as there may be information provided by the applicant which has the ability to alter the original decision. The guidance sets out some examples of what information may be capable of changing the decision on review. Such circumstances include those where a perpetrator of anti-social behaviour has left the household. Many allocation schemes will have provisions within them that disqualify those where there has been anti-social behaviour and/or will factor such matters in when determining priorities/giving reasonable preference. As such, if an original decision has been made based upon the anti-social behaviour of someone within an applicant's household and on review there is evidence that member of the household is no longer to be part of the application and household, then it is clear to see why a review decision might have a different, and more favourable, outcome for the applicant and their remaining household.

(f) Deadline for reviews. Eight weeks is suggested as a reasonable timescale for a local housing authority to conduct a review. The statutory guidance for local authorities encourages reviews to be completed, where possible, within a set timeframe with a specific deadline. Where an extension is required, the local housing authority should inform the applicant giving any explanation (*i.e.* its reasons) as to why it needs an extension. An extension may be required in circumstances where, for example, medical evidence is taking longer to obtain than the timeframe allows.

(g) Notification of the outcome of the review. The review decision must be given in writing to the applicant. Reasons for the decision must be set out. If the decision is lengthy, it is good practice to use paragraph numbers (and (sub)headings if the decision allows for a such a stricture). Basic techniques like these make it easier for an applicant to understand and follow but will also assist both

> sides and the court should any decision be challenged. The decision should be as clear as possible and deal with all the matters that raised by the applicant.

It is important to recognise that there may be cases that require a certain amount of flexibility when a local housing authority is handling them. It is good, therefore, for authorities to be able to maintain a discretion, particularly on the basis of exceptional circumstances, on all aspects of the review process. This should allow the authority to adapt its processes for very specific, and perhaps unforeseen, circumstances which may arise.

Repeat applications

Where a local housing authority come to a negative decision that an application does not qualify for an allocation of social housing, if the applicant can demonstrate that their circumstances have changed, they can make a new application.[198]

---

[198] Section 160ZA(11) and *Allocation of accommodation: guidance for local authorities*, Department for Levelling Up, Housing and Communities, published 29 June 2012 and updated 15 May 2023 at paragraph 3.36.

MORE BOOKS BY LAW BRIEF PUBLISHING

A selection of our other titles available now:-

'A Practical Guide to the Independent School Standards – September 2023 Edition' by Sarah McKimm
'A Practical Guide to Estate Administration and Crypto Assets' by Richard Marshall
'A Practical Guide to Managing GDPR Data Subject Access Requests – Second Edition' by Patrick O'Kane
'A Practical Guide to Parental Alienation in Private and Public Law Children Cases' by Sam King QC & Frankie Shama
'Contested Heritage – Removing Art from Land and Historic Buildings' by Richard Harwood QC, Catherine Dobson, David Sawtell
'The Limits of Separate Legal Personality: When Those Running a Company Can Be Held Personally Liable for Losses Caused to Third Parties Outside of the Company' by Dr Mike Wilkinson
'A Practical Guide to Transgender Law' by Robin Moira White & Nicola Newbegin
'A Practical Guide to 'Stranded Spouses' in Family Law' by Mani Singh Basi
'A Practical Guide to Residential Freehold Conveyancing' by Lorraine Richardson
'A Practical Guide to Pensions on Divorce for Lawyers' by Bryan Scant
'A Practical Guide to Challenging Sham Marriage Allegations in Immigration Law' by Priya Solanki
'A Practical Guide to Digital Communications Evidence in Criminal Law' by Sam Willis
'A Practical Guide to Legal Rights in Scotland' by Sarah-Jane Macdonald
'A Practical Guide to New Build Conveyancing' by Paul Sams & Rebecca East
'A Practical Guide to Defending Barristers in Disciplinary Cases' by Marc Beaumont
'A Practical Guide to Inherited Wealth on Divorce' by Hayley Trim
'A Practical Guide to Practice Direction 12J and Domestic Abuse in Private Law Children Proceedings' by Rebecca Cross & Malvika Jaganmohan

'A Practical Guide to Confiscation and Restraint' by Narita Bahra QC, John Carl Townsend, David Winch
'A Practical Guide to the Law of Forests in Scotland' by Philip Buchan
'A Practical Guide to Health and Medical Cases in Immigration Law' by Rebecca Chapman & Miranda Butler
'A Practical Guide to Bad Character Evidence for Criminal Practitioners by Aparna Rao
'A Practical Guide to Extradition Law post-Brexit' by Myles Grandison et al
'A Practical Guide to Hoarding and Mental Health for Housing Lawyers' by Rachel Coyle
'A Practical Guide to Psychiatric Claims in Personal Injury – 2nd Edition' by Liam Ryan
'Stephens on Contractual Indemnities' by Richard Stephens
'A Practical Guide to the EU Succession Regulation' by Richard Frimston
'A Practical Guide to Solicitor and Client Costs – 2nd Edition' by Robin Dunne
'Constructive Dismissal – Practice Pointers and Principles' by Benjimin Burgher
'A Practical Guide to Religion and Belief Discrimination Claims in the Workplace' by Kashif Ali
'A Practical Guide to the Law of Medical Treatment Decisions' by Ben Troke
'Fundamental Dishonesty and QOCS in Personal Injury Proceedings: Law and Practice' by Jake Rowley
'A Practical Guide to the Law in Relation to School Exclusions' by Charlotte Hadfield & Alice de Coverley
'A Practical Guide to Divorce for the Silver Separators' by Karin Walker
'The Right to be Forgotten – The Law and Practical Issues' by Melissa Stock
'A Practical Guide to Planning Law and Rights of Way in National Parks, the Broads and AONBs' by James Maurici QC, James Neill et al
'A Practical Guide to Election Law' by Tom Tabori
'A Practical Guide to the Law in Relation to Surrogacy' by Andrew Powell
'A Practical Guide to Claims Arising from Fatal Accidents – 2nd Edition' by James Patience
'A Practical Guide to the Ownership of Employee Inventions – From Entitlement to Compensation' by James Tumbridge & Ashley Roughton
'A Practical Guide to Asbestos Claims' by Jonathan Owen & Gareth McAloon

'A Practical Guide to Stamp Duty Land Tax in England and Northern Ireland' by Suzanne O'Hara
'A Practical Guide to the Law of Farming Partnerships' by Philip Whitcomb
'Covid-19, Homeworking and the Law – The Essential Guide to Employment and GDPR Issues' by Forbes Solicitors
'Covid-19 and Criminal Law – The Essential Guide' by Ramya Nagesh
'Covid-19 and Family Law in England and Wales – The Essential Guide' by Safda Mahmood
'A Practical Guide to the Law of Unlawful Eviction and Harassment – 2nd Edition' by Stephanie Lovegrove
'Covid-19, Brexit and the Law of Commercial Leases – The Essential Guide' by Mark Shelton
'A Practical Guide to Costs in Personal Injury Claims – 2nd Edition' by Matthew Hoe
'A Practical Guide to the General Data Protection Regulation (GDPR) – 2nd Edition' by Keith Markham
'Ellis on Credit Hire – Sixth Edition' by Aidan Ellis & Tim Kevan
'A Practical Guide to Working with Litigants in Person and McKenzie Friends in Family Cases' by Stuart Barlow
'Protecting Unregistered Brands: A Practical Guide to the Law of Passing Off' by Lorna Brazell
'A Practical Guide to Secondary Liability and Joint Enterprise Post-Jogee' by Joanne Cecil & James Mehigan
'A Practical Guide to the Pre-Action RTA Claims Protocol for Personal Injury Lawyers' by Antonia Ford
'A Practical Guide to Neighbour Disputes and the Law' by Alexander Walsh
'A Practical Guide to Forfeiture of Leases' by Mark Shelton
'A Practical Guide to Coercive Control for Legal Practitioners and Victims' by Rachel Horman
'A Practical Guide to the Law of Driverless Cars – Second Edition' by Alex Glassbrook, Emma Northey & Scarlett Milligan
'A Practical Guide to TOLATA Claims' by Greg Williams
'A Practical Guide to Elderly Law – 2nd Edition' by Justin Patten
'A Practical Guide to Responding to Housing Disrepair and Unfitness Claims' by Iain Wightwick

'A Practical Guide to the Law of Bullying and Harassment in the Workplace' by Philip Hyland

'How to Be a Freelance Solicitor: A Practical Guide to the SRA-Regulated Freelance Solicitor Model' by Paul Bennett

'A Practical Guide to Prison Injury Claims' by Malcolm Johnson

'A Practical Guide to the Small Claims Track – 2nd Edition' by Dominic Bright

'A Practical Guide to Advising Clients at the Police Station' by Colin Stephen McKeown-Beaumont

'A Practical Guide to Antisocial Behaviour Injunctions' by Iain Wightwick

'Practical Mediation: A Guide for Mediators, Advocates, Advisers, Lawyers, and Students in Civil, Commercial, Business, Property, Workplace, and Employment Cases' by Jonathan Dingle with John Sephton

'The Mini-Pupillage Workbook' by David Boyle

'A Practical Guide to Crofting Law' by Brian Inkster

'A Practical Guide to the Law of Domain Names and Cybersquatting' by Andrew Clemson

'A Practical Guide to the Law of Gender Pay Gap Reporting' by Harini Iyengar

'NHS Whistleblowing and the Law' by Joseph England

'Employment Law and the Gig Economy' by Nigel Mackay & Annie Powell

'A Practical Guide to Noise Induced Hearing Loss (NIHL) Claims' by Andrew Mckie, Ian Skeate, Gareth McAloon

'An Introduction to Beauty Negligence Claims – A Practical Guide for the Personal Injury Practitioner' by Greg Almond

'Intercompany Agreements for Transfer Pricing Compliance' by Paul Sutton

'Zen and the Art of Mediation' by Martin Plowman

'A Practical Guide to the SRA Principles, Individual and Law Firm Codes of Conduct 2019 – What Every Law Firm Needs to Know' by Paul Bennett

'A Practical Guide to Adoption for Family Lawyers' by Graham Pegg

'A Practical Guide to Industrial Disease Claims' by Andrew Mckie & Ian Skeate

'A Practical Guide to Conducting a Sheriff Court Proof' by Andrew Stevenson

'A Practical Guide to Vicarious Liability' by Mariel Irvine

'A Practical Guide to Applications for Landlord's Consent and Variation of Leases' by Mark Shelton

'A Practical Guide to Relief from Sanctions Post-Mitchell and Denton' by Peter Causton

'A Practical Guide to Equity Release for Advisors' by Paul Sams
'A Practical Guide to Financial Services Claims' by Chris Hegarty
'The Law of Houses in Multiple Occupation: A Practical Guide to HMO Proceedings' by Julian Hunt
'Occupiers, Highways and Defective Premises Claims: A Practical Guide Post-Jackson – 2nd Edition' by Andrew Mckie
'A Practical Guide to Financial Ombudsman Service Claims' by Adam Temple & Robert Scrivenor
'A Practical Guide to Running Housing Disrepair and Cavity Wall Claims: 2nd Edition' by Andrew Mckie & Ian Skeate
'A Practical Guide to Holiday Sickness Claims – 2nd Edition' by Andrew Mckie & Ian Skeate
'Arguments and Tactics for Personal Injury and Clinical Negligence Claims' by Dorian Williams
'A Practical Guide to Drone Law' by Rufus Ballaster, Andrew Firman, Eleanor Clot
'A Practical Guide to Compliance for Personal Injury Firms Working With Claims Management Companies' by Paul Bennett
'RTA Allegations of Fraud in a Post-Jackson Era: The Handbook – 2nd Edition' by Andrew Mckie
'RTA Personal Injury Claims: A Practical Guide Post-Jackson' by Andrew Mckie
'On Experts: CPR35 for Lawyers and Experts' by David Boyle
'An Introduction to Personal Injury Law' by David Boyle

These books and more are available to order online direct from the publisher at www.lawbriefpublishing.com, where you can also read free sample chapters. For any queries, contact us on 0844 587 2383 or mail@lawbriefpublishing.com.

Our books are also usually in stock at www.amazon.co.uk with free next day delivery for Prime members, and at good legal bookshops such as Wildy & Sons.

We are regularly launching new books in our series of practical day-to-day practitioners' guides. Visit our website and join our free newsletter to be kept informed and to receive special offers, free chapters, etc.

You can also follow us on Twitter at www.twitter.com/lawbriefpub.

www.ingramcontent.com/pod-product-compliance
Lightning Source LLC
LaVergne TN
LVHW022109200926
848481LV00003B/1113
9781916698079